Sgt. Sargent's TRENTON

J. William Sargent

HANGAR BOOKS

Canadian Cataloguing in Publication Data

Sargent, J. William, (James William), 1914 -
   Sgt. Sargent's Trenton

ISBN 0-920497-06-3

1. Canada RCAF Station (Trenton, Ont.)
- History. 2. Sgt., J. William, (James William), 1914 -
3. Air bases, Canadian - Social Life and customs.
4. World war, 1939 - 1945 - Personal narrative,
Canadian.

UG635.C32T75 1985 358.4'11292 C85-099068-8

© J. William Sargent, 1985
Published by: The Hangar Bookshelf
            Box 1513 Belleville, Ont. K8N 5J2
Printed and bound by, John Deyell Company.

Contents

1. Preface 6
2. The Road to Trenton 8
3. Plucking Square Pegs from Round Holes 11
4. The Early CONTACTs 13
5. And They Shall Have Music 18
6. On the Flying Side 25
7. Musing About The Muse 32
8. Station Warrant Officer John Silver 39
9. Something New in Blue 43
10. The New CONTACT 49
11. On the Waterfront 57
12. Four Commanding Officers 63
13. G/C T.A. Lawrence 65
14. G/C F.S. McGill 67
15. G/C R.E. McBurney 69
16. G/C A.D. Bell-Irving 71
17. Pin-Ups and Cover Girls 73
18. Cpl Rene Kulbach — Muralist Extraordinary 79
19. The International Scene 83
20. Fight Nights 87
21. Some Valiant Men 91
22. Flight Sergeant Eric Nicol 97
23. Preparing For After the Brawl 101
24. Do Some Cartoons 107
25. Victory Bonds for Victory 115
26. Cpl Alex "Wrong-way" Lebskin 119
27. Troupers at Trenton 125
28. Off the Base 129
29. A Potpourri of Memorabilia 133
30. Epilogue 141

Foreword

It was with pleasure that I agreed to comment on "Sgt Sargent's Trenton", a draft of which I read with delight and great interest. Here is a book that many airforce and ex-airforce personnel who did not get overseas have been looking for — that is, a collection of stories about a Canadian RCAF training base in wartime. The title itself makes it immediately obvious that the book is based on an NCO's experience, to which those thousands who served in the other ranks can relate. Yet it will also be of interest to officers at all levels who wish to know what went on in that vast substructure from which their rank or position barred them.

Written in an easy-to-read style with good flow - and including amusing anecdotes as well as relevant and historical material - the stories will recall for readers their own station life and their own special people, wherever they served. Ex-Airwomen will, I think, welcome "Sgt Sargent's Trenton". Not many books about the RCAF have given space to activities of the Women's Division but this one is generous with both its editorial and photographic pages.

For me, the book brought back many nostalgic memories and recalls names and events I had forgotten. It will do the same for many readers, I'm sure.

Air Vice Marshal R.E. McBurney

Preface

It was mid-1945. The war in Europe was over and RCAF Trenton's magazine, CONTACT, marked the event with a special VE Souvenir Number. The cover photograph was of His Majesty King George VI in the uniform of a marshal of the Royal Air Force.

On page three, Corporal Rene Kulbach, an RCAF service policeman who was also one of Canada's finest muralists, had contributed an interesting illustration depicting the part which Trenton had played in the defeat of our enemies. Within the illustration I had written this message:

"From five-and-a-half years of war, the Royal Canadian Air Force at Trenton has emerged a great teacher.

In its skies, young men of all nations have been taught the perfection of flying, while on the ground their brothers and sisters have learned the skill with which to administer a mighty air training plan.

From this vast university they have gone forth to throw their strength against the enemy, some to win glory in the battle skies of Europe, others to build the foundation for overwhelming air power at the Dominion's training schools.

Today, in this hour of triumph and rededication to the cause of freedom, Trenton proudly lifts its head, for victory is a monument to the success of its mighty undertaking."

It is not my intention to elaborate on the wartime achievements of the Royal Canadian Air Force at Trenton, some of which have been admirably recorded in the Anniversary book, *"Trenton - Fifty Years of Air Force"* ... and elsewhere.

Rather, the purpose of this book is to report on the lighter side of wartime Trenton — to tell something about the interesting and often amusing activities of men and women who made up the base. I saw and often reported on these activities — first as art editor of the wartime CONTACT and later as its editor.

Parts of some of the stories told here were presented in various forms in wartime issues of the station paper. Quite often, there were sides to stories which, for quite understandable reasons in those days, went unpublished. In a number of such stories I have corrected this. While the book may appear, sometimes, to be too concerned with the operation of the station paper, this is unavoidable. CONTACT was the chronicler of activities on the base and it was the ideal vantage point from which to learn about and view a wide range of events.

There may be some readers who were at Trenton during World War II whose views of activities then may differ from my own — for not everybody sees the same situations in the same light. The passage of time can dim the memory, also. My views, necessitated by my responsibility to the station paper, were made when I was cold sober and my memory has been refreshed by the complete volumes of wartime CONTACT in my possession. The stories tell of many people — and cover many events that occurred at Trenton from the time I arrived at the base in late 1941 until I was discharged and left the air station in October 1945.

For some time before the base's 50th Anniversary Celebrations in 1981, the then CONTACT editor, Joan Wright, saw fit to republish some of the wartime stories under the heading, "Those Were The Days". Since then, she has given space under the same heading to more recent contributions of mine. Her remark that present-day personnel, as well as past Trentonians, find the stories interesting is one of my excuses for writing this book. Another reason is the number of letters which appear in AIRFORCE magazine from readers wanting stories about Canadian bases. These appear to be from ex-airforce personnel who were among the four out of every five RCAF men and women who did not get overseas. Unable to relate to the glamorous stories of operations overseas, they feel a bit left out of things because they were ground or aircrew in Canada. Yet they are proud to have served in the RCAF and wish, now and then, for a little recognition.

J. William Sargent

About reading this Book: The first 3 chapters should be read in sequence, for they set the scene. The remaining chapters may be read in any order, for each is a separate story.

The Road to Trenton

Quite frankly, I had not heard of Trenton Air Station when I entered the RCAF in 1941 as potential aircrew. My friend, Bill Collard, and I had applied for enlistment and one day we were ordered to a Recruiting Office on Bay Street in Toronto. There, as the eldest in a group of thirteen recruits, I was told to take us all — complete with RCAF armbands and documents — to a Manning Depot at St. Hubert, near Montreal, Quebec. The Manning Depot at Toronto, we were told, was full up.

I had never been in charge of men before but learned something about what it is like during the train ride to Montreal. At almost every railway stop one or more of my group left the train to phone home to Mom or somebody and report on the progress we were making. I worried about them getting back to the train on time — and what would happen to me if I arrived at St. Hubert minus a few bodies.

At the Windsor Station in Montreal, we were headed down the platform when we ran smack into another group of young men, each wearing an RCAF armband.

"Where are you fellows going?" we yelled in unison, hoping that they, too, were headed for St. Hubert.

"We're going to the Toronto Manning Depot," they hollered back. "The one here is full up."

We became concerned about the outcome of the war.

A truck driver from St. Hubert appeared on the scene and drove us to the Manning Depot where I lined up my group and reported to an officer that I had arrived from Toronto with thirteen recruits. He looked us over.

"You've got fourteen," he advised.

I had, too. Questioning disclosed that a recruit had boarded the train at Kingston, Ontario and, seeing our armbands, had joined us.

The officer said something funny about sending me out again as a recruiter and then told us that there were no tents for us — just tent floorboards. We were to take empty palliase cases to a pile of straw, fill them and use them as mattresses as we slept under the stars that night. The stars didn't show up — but a violent rainstorm did. This brought about a mad stampede, with clothes and blankets, to the nearest barracks where we were met by some awful language from the hut's awakened and startled denizens.

A few days later we were transferred by train to another depot at Valcartier, Quebec. Valcartier was a huge army camp but the RCAF had taken over some territory and huts to establish a Manning Depot there. No uniforms had been issued to us to this point but this did not stop some of the powers-that-be at Valcartier, mostly corporals, from putting us on parade.

Right from the very start, my friend Bill was a standout on parade, mainly because of the white civilian shoes he was wearing.

Gradually, piecemeal, we were issued uniforms — abeit, ill-fitting in many cases.

Some of us were selected to serve in a precision drill squad — for it was announced that His Royal Highness The Duke of Kent would be inspecting the Depot soon and everybody was expected to put on a good show. We were marched and drilled endlessly between barrack huts and on an earthen parade area. Our proficiency increased rapidly — as did the amount of mud we marched through ... for the rain we thought we had left behind at St. Hubert had followed us to Valcartier and decided to stay there. The parade area became a quagmire.

Finally, the great day came. We lined up in the mud under more rain. After what seemed like hours it was announced that His Royal Highness would not be coming after all. It was too wet. We had just become familiar with the RCAF phrase — "a dim view." It seemed like an apt one to take on this occasion so, collectively, we took it.

Our next big day was when we were shipped off to Initial Training School at Victoriaville, Quebec, where we became members of Course No. 35. This was more like it. It was at ITS that I first heard the word "Trenton". It was not exactly a swearword — more like the proper noun that it is but always preceded or followed by a fair amount of profanity. From members of Course No. 34 who had flunked out, we learned why. Trenton was their next destination. They were headed for the Aircrew Reselection Centre — otherwise known as the "washed-out aircrew pool." To potential aircrew the name Trenton brought disappointment and despondency — as I was soon to find out after a session in the ITS hospital. Discharge saw me recategorized as "medically unfit for aircrew" — and I was on my way to Trenton.

The Road to Trenton / 9

Above: Trenton by night, 1944. Note lights of taxiing aircraft and No. 6 Repair Depot in background.

Right: an evening view of the water tower, a base landmark and sentinel. The light atop of it continuously serves as a beacon sending out the identifying dah-T dahdit-N, seen on a clear night for 30 miles. The top also contained "Wailing Willie," the annoying siren that doubled as an alarm clock and a "Lights out" warning.

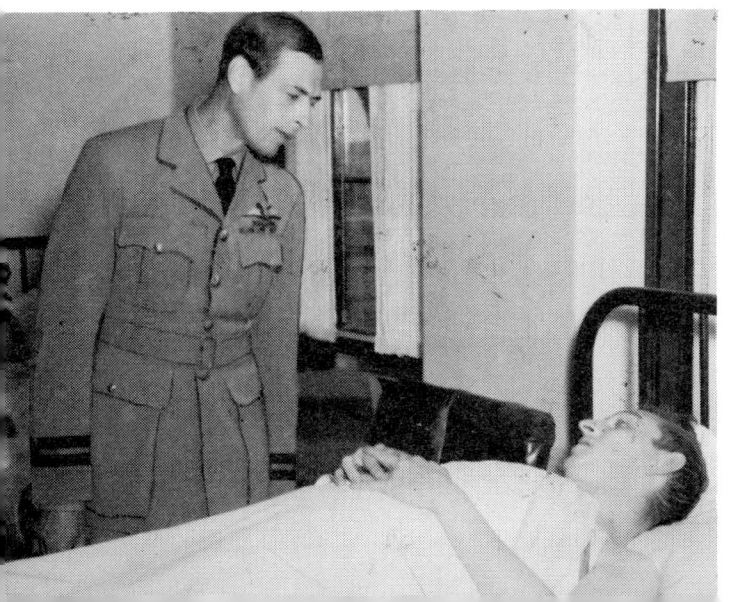

Left: Air Commodore HRH The Duke of Kent, who visited the base in 1941, is shown talking to a hospital patient. A year later, His Royal Highness was killed in a flying accident while serving in the line of duty.

Plucking Square Pegs from Round Holes

Many potential pilots and observers sent to Trenton for reselection to other aircrew or ground trades arrived full of apprehension. Trenton was a huge place. It was bustling with thousands of airmen. It had a reputation for spit and polish. Some weird stories about the place had circulated throughout the air training schools. There was uncertainty about one's future. There were no airwomen there.

My destination was the Composite Training School — otherwise known as KTS to avoid confusion with another Trenton unit, CFS (Central Flying School) and the CTS (Conversion Training Squadron) at Rockcliffe, Ontario.

KTS, under the command of W/C H.J. Burden, was comprised of two squadrons — the Training Squadron and the Aircrew Reselection Squadron. The job of the Training Squadron was to teach and graduate clerks, service policemen, firemen, disciplinarians, motorboat crewmen, physical training instructors and others to serve in the scores of schools of the British Commonwealth Air Training Plan. Staff and students in the Training Squadron went about their jobs conscientiously and enthusiastically. In the main, they knew what had to be done and the students had some idea of where they might be going upon graduation.

Staff of the Aircrew Squadron were also efficient and dedicated but squadron similarities ended there. As well as being apprehensive, men headed for the Aircrew Squadron arrived at Trenton angry and dispirited. There were, I believe, about 1,000 of us awaiting reselection at any one time during the early years of the war. There was a continuous turnover as some men left after being assigned to other aircrew or ground trades — while other grounded types arrived from ITS, EFTS and SFTS

Plucking Square Pegs from Round Holes / 11

establishments.* Morale was low — and raising it was an early objective of the staff. Trenton was well equipped with both men and facilities for this purpose.

While awaiting appointments with interviewing officers, medical officers and trade test officers there was always physical training, drill and studies related to flying to occupy some of our time. The idea was to combat boredom and I can remember being taken with groups to the station's movie houses on several occasions. There were, we were told, all kinds of recreational facilities at Trenton — and this has always been true of the base. Nothing was said to us, when we arrived, about snow shovelling. Things may have changed but during the war years Trenton seemed to receive more than its fair share of snow. The Reselection Centre became a handy reservoir of shovellers.

Regardless of the recreational facilities, movies and snow shovelling, many of us were still bored stiff while waiting to appear before the various boards.

The officer commanding the Aircrew Reselection Squadron was Squadron Leader Denton Massey of the famous farm machinery family, cousin to the famed movie star, Raymond, and to our future Governor General, Vincent. In civilian life, S/L Massey had had ample opportunities to work with young men through his well-known and remarkable religious institution, the York Bible Class. This Bible class not only drew enormous numbers of young men to its services but the services themselves were broadcast by radio over much of Canada.

One day, it was my turn to go before the trade test officer. I had previously seen all kinds of signs, crudely handwritten, tacked onto doors of various offices. The sight offended me for in civilian life I had taken an extension course in elementary commercial art and, therefore, thought I knew a good sign from a bad one. To the trade test officer, I said: "I'm bored stiff. If anybody has pen and ink I can do better signs than you have around here."

"Can you draw?" he asked.

I replied that I could draw a bit — whereupon the officer picked up a phone and called somebody at Station Headquarters.

"We've got a lad here who can draw," he said, "Can you use him?"

Somebody apparently could and I was sent up to the Administration Building. RCAF Trenton was about to start its own printed magazine and I was to be its full-time artist. It was the trade test officer's coup d'etat for I not only served my RCAF time on the station paper — the next 34 years of my life were spent in the publishing business.

*Initial Training Schools,
Elementary Flying Training Schools and
Service Flying Training Schools.

The Early CONTACTS

It was not until the occupation of the Rhineland by British, French and American armies after the First World War that the first modern newsheets were established and printed by and for the troops. In the Second World War the earliest attempts to provide newspapers for the forces were in the western desert where the Eighth Army had its own paper.

At RCAF Station, Trenton, the first issue of CONTACT was published in November 1940. It was an eleven-page publication, typewritten and printed by mimeograph on foolscap paper. It had been started by Sergeant Major Dick Sherwood and Corporal Ed Lally. Thanks to a generous donor at the Station's 50th Anniversary Celebrations in 1981, I have a rare copy of this historic issue. From November 1940, Trenton's Commanding Officer was Group Captain T.A. Lawrence and it was he who wanted a publication befitting the importance of Trenton as the heart of the British Commonwealth Air Training Plan — a printed magazine with colour, photographs and other illustrations. Work on the first issue started in late 1941 and some of the early, inevitable obstructions were cleared away through the efforts of the Station Administration Officer, Wing Commander H.H. Atkinson, who was, in fact, Canada's No. 1 airman. He had joined the Canadian Air Force on the last day of May, 1920 and had been given the regimental number "One".

There is no record of who named the publication — but the name was apt. The word "Contact" had been connected with aviation for many years. It was a verbal instruction exchanged between the pilot and his groundcrew when the engine was about to be started. The name was apt according to a dictionary definition, too, i.e. — the establishing of communication.

When I visited the Trenton base during the 1981 celebrations it surprised me to learn that young men and women there had no idea that the name of their station paper had ever been an aviation term. I tried to explain the similarity of starting an airplane engine in the old days to turning the crank of an automobile to start the engine — but, of course, they didn't know about that either. The matter became the subject of an editorial in CONTACT's forty-four-page Air Show Issue published in September 1981. The fact that an explanation was necessary indicates that time no longer marches on — it jets on.

While nobody knows who named the publication there is on record the fact the very smart distinctive cover of the 1942 CONTACTS was designed by Pilot Officer J.C. Hood.

The first issue of the printed 1942 CONTACT, published in January, was lined up by Flying Officer Guy Lafleur, a former Montreal newspaperman, but he was posted before completion of the issue. His position as managing editor was taken over by F/O E.T. Hamilton, an American. F/O Hamilton had worked in civilian life on such well-known U.S. publications as Cosmopolitan and Liberty. The editor was Sgt Fred Rogers. The rest of the staff consisted of anybody with experience (and me with no experience) who could be plucked out of Maintenance Wing, Headquarters and the Aircrew Reselection Centre, which always seemed to be able to come up with some ex-journalists. The plan for the first six issues called for presentation of an interesting pictorial and editorial cross-section of the Station, each number dwelling on one particular unit such as Central Flying School, Composite Training School, Headquarters and so on.

Among the part-time contributors in the early days was AC1 Stan Helleur of Maintenance Wing who was not only a fine writer but an accomplished illustrator as well. In late May of 1942, Stan became both editor and managing editor when F/O Hamilton transferred to the U.S. Air Force. Other contributors were LAC Metcalfe of KTS, LAC John (RAF), and LAC John Newbold (formerly of The Toronto Star). LAC Don Richardson of Headquarters was in charge of circulation. Richardson liked to report that his chief claim to fame was introduction into the Wet Canteen of a drink called a Molson's Float (a scoop of ice cream in a glass of ale). The drink never caught on.

One of the prime requisites for publishing CONTACT in printed form was money — and this was obtained by selling advertising space to shops and firms in the surrounding districts. Our advertising manager was LAC Jack Pennylegion, a portly airman with enthusiasm and selling skills to match his size. We were all envious of Jack because his work took him off the base so much. We saw even less of him when somebody came up with the bright idea of selling advertising space to resort hotels in Ontario's beautiful Muskoka Lakes holiday district. Jack's job was to convince resort owners that they should surround a CONTACT map of the area with advertisements enticing airmen to spend leaves at their respective establishments. To do this, Jack had to visit the resorts. He stayed at some and no doubt engaged in many of the resort activities. We thought it had to be the best job of the war — anywhere.

Of course, the editor enjoyed some nice trips, too. I could never understand, at first, why we had to have the magazine

14 / The Early Contacts

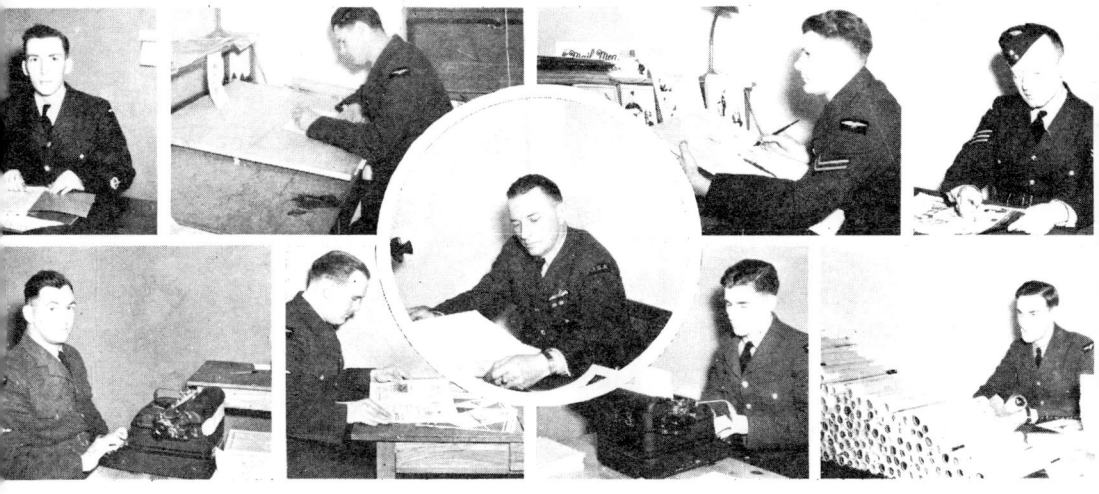

Staff of the first printed CONTACTS. Gathered from all over the base, they were: centre: F/O E.T. Hamilton, CFS; clockwise from top left: WO2 C. Simmons, Hdqts; AC1 S. Helleur, CFS; Cpl J.W. Sargent, Hdqts; Sgt. F.A. Rogers, Hdqts; LAC D. Richardson, Hdqts. LAC I. John, KTS; LAC J. Pennylegion, Hdqts; LAC J. Newbold, KTS;

The well-known Administration Building, in front of which was the main parade square.

Members of the RN Fleet Air Arm, assigned to the Aircrew Reselection Centre, lead a 1942 march past the saluting base.

F/L R.K. Cameron leads some of the personnel of FIS, CFS and Maintenance Wings during a 1944 church service held in No. 6 Hangar.

printed at Gardenvale, Quebec when there were facilities closer by at Kingston and Toronto. I later learned there were feminine attractions as well as printing presses at Gardenvale. Not all planning went into winning of the war.

April 1942 saw a change of command take place at Trenton, with Group Captain F.S. McGill replacing G/C Lawrence. The magazine itself was also undergoing a change as the last of the issues covering descriptions of the units and their staffs was published in June. From then on the publication took on a different appearance with much larger photographs, a more modern layout and a content featuring the more general activities of the base.

I also had taken on a new look when two stripes were put up on the sleeves of my tunic. I became Corporal Sargent — and this odd combination of rank and name, followed later by Sergeant Sargent and Flight Sergeant Sargent, plagued me from then on until the end of the war. One day, I picked up a ringing telephone and announced:

"Corporal Sargent here."

There was a pause at the other end of the line — then an officer from the flying field roared...

"Don't you know what the hell you are? Are you a corporal or sergeant?"

I explained that I was both and began to sympathize with another NCO whose name was Major. We both felt better when an airman with an even more interesting combination of rank and name arrived on the station.

He was an AC2 — an aircraftsman, second class. His name was A.C. Tew so he immediately became known as AC2 A.C. Tew. This oddity became a news item in CONTACT, appeared the following year in the national publication WINGS, and even popped up as an item now and then in daily newspapers across Canada.

The magazine was going great guns and a lot of new and important things were happening on the base in 1942. September saw the first contingent of about 200 airwomen, known as WDs, arrive on the station. We were told to not only give the arrival a fair amount of publicity but also ordered to turn over two or three pages for specific news about airwomen from then on. The main page of this section was headed "What's Doin' " — with the emphasis on the capitals W and D, the initials standing for an abbreviation of Women's Division. An editor, AW2 Edith Motley, was chosen. Whether or not she wrote the column "Introducing the Girls", I can't recall, but in this column the writer set about describing some of the more prominent or popular airwomen.

In one of the early issues, a girl who was working as a cook in the station hospital was described as having "wide-set blue eyes and even teeth." When the printer's proof arrived, the description had become — "She's the girl with the side-set blue eyes and even teeth." The proof was returned with instructions that the letter "s" in front of "ide" be taken out and replaced by the letter "w". We didn't see a corrected proof and were stunned when the magazine came out. We found that the "s" which was to have been deleted had somehow found its way over to the front of the word "even". So the description then read ... "She's the girl with the wide-set blue eyes and seven teeth."

Knowing that women can become pretty touchy about this type of goof, a hurried staff meeting was held. We reached a decision that the time might be as good as any for the editor to go on an immediate leave. Which I believe he did.

But like many good things, CONTACT was coming to an end. Or so it seemed. An air force headquarters ruling from Ottawa prohibited the selling of advertising after December 1, 1942. No advertising meant no paper. Station publications like CONTACT had been making too substantial inroads into the advertising budgets of business concerns, thereby depriving newspapers, chiefly those in smaller towns and cities, from advertising income they otherwise would receive. It made sense.

CONTACT, however, was not about to pass out of the picture with a whimper. Air Commodore McGill ordered that the final December issue be a special one in every way. And it was. Eighty-four pages thick, it featured photographs of every member of every staff on the station.

Station papers were supposed to be replaced by a new Ottawa headquarters publication called WINGS. It was to be a Sunday supplement type of publication, liberally supplied with cartoons and feature stories from all over Canada. Trenton's editor, Stan Helleur, was lifted from the station and posted to Ottawa to help get it started.

Less than three months later the situation changed. The first issues of WINGS, beautifully presented and professionally produced, were not doing the job the station papers did. While providing an excellent picture of the RCAF in Canada and worldwide, WINGS could not give space to the very personal news items so popular with station personnel. Airmen and airwomen were not so interested in what was going on at other bases as they were in what was happening on their own.

CONTACT was among the first of a number of air force publications that quickly adapted to this new situation. A new, less elaborate station paper arose — but that is another story.

And They Shall Have Music

Music at Trenton was many things. Like the Saracens and crusaders of centuries ago we had our bands — brass, trumpet and bagpipe. But music at Trenton was more than that — more than marching and parade square music. It was music in almost every known form — soothing and stirring classics emanating from "music appreciation hours" held in the station library ... happy sounds from harmonicas, guitars and accordions played by airmen for their barracks mates ... the sweet song of a WD entertaining at a station concert ... the strident, sometimes smooth big band sound bursting through the confines of the Sports Hangar as men and women danced to the rhythmic beat ... the full-throated sound of men's and women's voices lifted reverently in song at church parades ... the raucous shouting, singing in the wet canteens. It was this and more.

But if martial music is what most people associate with military bases, Trenton was indeed fortunate — for we had fine bands. Before and during the first days of WWII, band personnel at Trenton consisted of tradesmen who took up their musical instruments after working hours and formed the nucleus of what was to become the official Trenton band. At that time, Trenton had the only RCAF band in Canada and, under WO2 Tommy Cooper, it left the base at one time to provide music at the Canadian National Exhibition. When war broke out postings so depleted the band's ranks that Ottawa enlisted bandsmen and sent them to Trenton as permanent replacements. For a while these, together with the tradesmen, played under the leadership of F/Sgt Stan McGuirl. Later, more regular bandsmen came, among them Ed Hancock, who became the bandmaster for most of Trenton's wartime years.

WO2 Hancock had been an experienced member of the Buffalo, Syracuse and Toronto symphony orchestras as well as a lead trombonist with the major-league U.S. dance band of Vincent Lopez. He took the station band up to a standard that made it an attraction both on and off the base. A pleasant cooperative man, he not only provided topnotch military music — he organized and produced many fine band concerts to entertain station personnel. As well, he composed Air Force march tunes, one of which, "Pilots of the RCAF", was aired to millions of Canadians and Americans over the CBS radio network in June 1942.

Trenton's trumpet band, like the original brass band, was formed entirely of volunteers. When it was organized by Cpl "Buck" Morland in May 1941, a full fifty percent of the players had never before had a drum or trumpet in their hands. Assisted by F/Sgt D.E. Burgess and Cpl P. Bisson of Central Flying School and Cpl Roger Prudhomme, the station's official trumpeter, Morland soon succeeded in building a band worthy of the great station. In exchange for their services, members were permitted to wear the smart white halyards of their profession and, because their practices had to be done at 7:30 a.m. morning sessions, the CO excused them from all duty watch and certain other station details. Postings were a headache to founder Morland but the problem was alleviated to some extent by the acquisition of some permanent drummer tradesmen and the promise of permanent trumpeters.

Towards the end of the 1942 summer, the trumpeters were equipped with new types of instruments, enabling them to combine with the brass band and play as one unit on several different occasions — producing such stirring music that few former Trentonians who marched to it will ever forget it. Mid-1943 saw Sgt Alex Davidson, the station band's cornet soloist, assist in formation of a WD trumpet band which, later, was merged with the men's band under the direction of Cpl Gordon Bender.

Although the moving sound of a full bagpipe band did not become part of Trenton until late in 1945, a lone piper was heard throughout most of the war years. He was F/Sgt Forbes Wilson, whose practicing could be heard in the very early hours of many mornings. Due to my discharge in October 1945, I was not able to enjoy for long the efforts of the fine kilted bagpipe band. I recall writing a feature story about it, though. It was formed by G/C E.G. Fullerton on his station at Summerside, P.E.I. The band eventually moved to Centralia before being posted to Trenton. G/C Fullerton was also responsible for the distinctive Air Force tartan used in the band's attractive uniforms. The pipe major was F/Sgt Tommy Carroll who had learned his piping skills in Canada's famous 48th Highlanders Band.

Where there were brass bands in the armed forces there were usually dance bands. In 1942, the "boogie-woogie" boys at Trenton were twelve solid gentlemen of swing under Stan McGuirl's direction — fellows happy to play for their love of music rather than their suppers. Most of their arrangements

Members of the Brass Band and Trumpet Band who formed the Combination Band in 1943 that was so popular.

Paul Raymond, former Montreal Canadien hockey star, shown running one of his Music Appreciation Hours in the station library.

Below left is F/Lt Wishart Campbell, well-known singer, entertaining at a station concert, while alongside are LAWs Elizabeth Porter and Dorothy Kinton, two airwomen who sang at many concerts.

WO2 Ed Hancock, station bandmaster and former member of symphonic orchestras and big name bands, who composed the march tune, "Pilots of the RCAF".

F/L Balfour, Wireless Section, who broadcast music from atop the water tower to the entire base.

Below: The colorful pipe band that came to the base in 1945 when No. 1 Air Command was formed. The featured piper is F/Sgt Tommy Carroll.

were Glen Miller's and the band was a smash hit at the every-other-week Station dances. The history of the dance orchestra is traceable back to the summer of 1939 when F/Sgt McDonald collaborated with F/O McKay to blend men and instruments into a smooth aggregation. A later orchestra leader was the popular F/O "Buff" Estes who also acted as master of ceremonies at a number of Station musical events. "Buff" had previously played with Benny Goodman's band.

But the band that Trentonians of the year 1944 will remember was the brilliant United States Army Air Force Band. Heralded as the finest military band in the world it arrived at Trenton on May 9 in five large Douglas aircraft — its mission to promote goodwill and comradeship between the U.S. and Canada. It held an audience of well over 4,000 air force personnel and civilians literally spellbound with an afternoon performance of symphonic and popular airs in the Sports Hangar — then traveled to No. 6 Repair Depot for a five o'clock performance. It then returned once more to the Sports Hangar to play for over 2,500 attending a big Victory Dance. The band had previously played before royalty and envoys from many countries. To gather this outstanding band, over 800 musicians were auditioned to obtain the 100 artists in the organization. It had, represented in its membership, thirty-two different symphonies including the New York Symphonic, the Philadelphia and others as equally world famous — and thirty-eight "Name Bands" included in which were Glen Miller, the Dorsey Brothers and Charlie Spivak.

In contrast to the large school of "ickies" or boogie-minded music lovers on the station, there were a substantial number of men and women who were more for the classics. And while the former could drop nickels into a jukebox and swing out every night, the "classics-addicts" had only two nights a week to howl during the early war years. The howling in this case was done at Music Appreciation Hours. It consisted of men and women relaxing in big leather chairs or settees in the library in the Airmen's Mess building, closing their eyes and thoroughly enjoying the soothing strains of a symphony or opera drift from the speaker of a combination radio phonograph. The Wednesday and Sunday night appreciation hours were the joint brainchild of Matt Keith, a YMCA supervisor, and LAC Walter Wright, an authority on good music or, as non-devotees called it, "that long-haired stuff." At first, records had to be borrowed but shortly after the popularity of the concerts was established, the Station Central Fund Committee coughed up funds which permitted records to be bought by the hundreds. Sometimes, to supplement the recordings, several guest artists appeared and proved popular.

No matter what the activity, postings were always a problem.

When LAC Wright and even the "Y" supervisor left, their places were taken over by others. Among some of the volunteers was padre F/L Ross Cameron who later, in civilian life, became Moderator of the Presbyterian Church in Canada. Another was LAC Paul Raymond, a former flashy forward for the Montreal Canadiens who, when not thinking about music in his spare time, was a tower of strength on the station hockey team.

There were a lot of great concerts at Trenton, some presented by outside entertainment groups performing as part of their volunteer war effort. The station itself, though, had a remarkable number of talented entertainers. In fact, they were so good that when the Canadian Broadcasting Corporation aired one of its famous "Comrades in Arms" radio broadcasts from the base, the CBC reported ... "This particular program in the series was voted the finest yet by the officers of the Service, heads of the CBC and members of the general public alike."

We had fine singers galore, so many we can't begin to name them all. Among the more notable male vocalists were Dr. S/L Harvie Doney and F/L Wishart Campbell, both popular in civilian life as radio stars. Sometimes there were impromptu concerts such as in the case of a young airman who sat down at a piano in the Airmen's Lounge one night, struck a few chords, then burst into a moving rendition of "The Lord's Prayer." The voice attracted a crowd and more songs were sung. The singer? LAC Denis Feeney, a highly-trained vocalist who had formerly been a principal in the International Opera Company at London's Covent Garden, and a recording star. Another favourite was F/Sgt Fred Phillips, a CBC baritone.

Female vocalists were also in abundance. Among the earliest and most popular in 1942 was AW1 Mary Gary, a star in the station's Rondelles Concert Party. Another very popular singer was LAW Dorothy Kinton who sang in concerts on and off the base, almost from the time of the airwomen's arrival at Trenton in '42 until well into 1945. In January 1945, the formation of No. 1 Air Command at the base brought with it LAW Elizabeth Porter, a young lady with a beautiful voice who, before and during the war, had been a highly regarded professional soprano in Toronto church choirs. After the war, she sang with the Canadian Opera Company, the well-known Carl Tapscott Singers, and the Festival Singers. There had to be accompanists, of course, and one of LAW Porter's was LAC Douglas Elliott, a fine musician and artist who, before leaving the air force, took the talented airwoman as his bride. They have lived in Toronto since the war. Among many other accompanists during the war were Cpl Frank Smithson and LAW Ella May White. The always obliging Ella May was sometimes recruited to play at the Officers' Mess. She lives in Burlington, Ontario, today.

There was always the other music — the barracks-room

And They Shall Have Music / 23

music. Everybody who served before, during and after the war will remember their own favourites. Some that I recall are F/Sgt "Pop" Fallis and his mouth organ, and guitarists LACs Cockburn and Mayhew. Formal glee clubs were in existence — one under the direction of LAC Bill Hill. And official singsongs were a feature of the WD barracks.

Abundant music — that was Trenton. In fact, even if one wanted to escape from music there was a time when it was well-nigh impossible.

It was mid-summer, 1944. F/L Balfour of the Wireless Section had decided there should be station-wide music during and after working hours, with a full Sunday evening presentation of semi-classical numbers. He and his staff installed, on top of the water tower, eight speakers — arranged so that their range covered the entire base. I don't know if the station had the title first or whether we pinched it from civilian radio stations, but our seventh-day evening program was called "Your Sunday Evening Serenade". A survey of the range disclosed that airmen in houses at the very far west end of the base could hear it. Nurses in the station hospital reported that patients inside the building also heard it. They liked the music and "even applauded after each number."

Airmen and airwomen walking down the main road were seen to stop and sit down on the lawns when the music started, ready to enjoy themselves and shed whatever cares they may have had, while listening to the hour or two of relaxing music. The situation cried out for one of the station paper's polls. To the question: "What do you think of the musical programs broadcast from the top of the water tower?" there was not one negative reply. In fact, many respondents took advantage of the poll to express preferences for different types of music — an unexpected editorial bonus which, when published, resulted in some spirited arguments in offices, messes and canteens.

Friedrich Nietzsche, the German philosopher stated: "Without music, life would be a mistake." He said it first but we at Trenton believed in the theory wholeheartedly — making sure, as much as possible, that our lives would be error-free.

On the Flying Side

From the inauguration of the British Commonwealth Air Training Plan in mid-October of 1939, Canada became the most important and largest training centre for airmen in the British Empire. By the time the final wings parades were being held across Canada on March 29th, 1945, 131,553 aircrew had been trained, included in which were 49,808 pilots.

Back of that tremendous effort stood the Flying Instructors School of RCAF Trenton — the very fountainhead from which ultimately sprang massive raids that pulverized the industrial centres of our enemies. Back in 1939, the first Flying Instructors School had been set up at Camp Borden where it was housed in six hangars and the old Air Force Headquarters building used in the First Great War. On January 19th, 1940, the FIS moved to Trenton and set some kind of record by continuing instructional classes just a day-and-a-half after the move.

The war, then in its second year, began to create a demand for instructors which far exceeded the supply and promised to call for still more as the Training Plan leapt ahead with unprecedented speed. Fifty aircraft, including all types, were put to use and in April 1940 the school's name was changed to Central Flying School to conform to RAF practice. Meanwhile, No. 6 Repair Depot, which had a staff of about 16 men and which was operating from the Sports Hangar, found itself in need of expansion. In late 1940, it became a separate station located in the northwest corner of the flying field.

When I arrived at Trenton in late 1941, the school was under the command of W/C G.P. Dunlop. The chief flying instructor was W/C F.C. Carling-Kelly and the officers commanding his two squadrons were S/L J.G. Stephenson and S/L J.G. Twist.

New hangars were being added to Trenton's fast growing flying setup and by October 1942 it was found necessary to reorganize CFS in order to satisfy the continually stepped-up demands of the BCATP. Prior to then, instructors were trained exclusively at Trenton but under the new setup CFS was divided into three FISs and four Visiting Flights. No. 1 FIS and the Visiting Flights, whose job it was to examine and recategorize instructors across Canada, were stationed at Trenton. The new setup had many advantages because it enabled each FIS to dwell

Central Flying School officers, 1942. Top left: W/C G.P. Dunlop, Officer Commanding. Above: W/C F.C. Carling-Kelly, Chief Flying Instructor. Left: S/L J.G. Twist, Officer Commanding No. 2 Squadron.

Above: S/L J.G. Stephenson, Officer Commanding, No. 1 Squadron.

Right: Winners, against other bases, of team bombing trophy, 1945. F/O E. Vollick receives trophy from A/V/M A.T.N. Cowley.

exclusively on one type of training, which permitted the turning out of more efficient instructors. It also increased production of instructors by approximately 800 more each year.

While instructors and potential instructors were busy in ground instruction classes and in the air, other men and, later, women were just as busy with the maintenance of aircraft and other essential ground work. This work required a wide variety of skilled persons, including aero-engine mechanics, airframe mechanics, instrument men, wireless mechanics, electricians, fabric workers, carpenters, sheetmetal workers and machinists.

By June 1944, there were close to 150 aircraft on the base, about three times as many as in April 1940. So there was plenty of work for all. Even checking sparkplugs kept people busy for there were eighteen plugs to every Harvard and many of the other aircraft were twin-engined.

In 1942 and, I imagine, throughout the war years, maintenance personnel were divided into two sections — those who handled aircraft in daily use by the flights and those engaged in repairs on grounded ships. Duties of the first included daily inspections of such items as tires, oleo legs, instruments, etc., and the provision of oil and gasoline. For more extensive inspections, for repairs of more than minor importance, aircraft were divided between those having single and those having twin engines.

Also on the flying side of the station were, of course, the ever-important control tower and meteorological experts, and the skilled men and women who packed parachutes.

My work took me across to the flying field only when asked to write stories about specific training or outstanding achievements — or to cadge a flip. Always noticeable to me on these occasions was not only the pride in workmanship in the hangars but also the good-natured rivalry and bantering between flights and sections. There was a trophy given monthly for the flight with the least number of accidents and I easily recall the expressions of pride and pleasure on the faces of officers and men as they formed up for the large photographs of winning flights we published in some 1942 CONTACTS.

On the bantering side I recall, particularly, the ribbing which WO2 Bob Cunningham, a CFS/FIS discip, bestowed on F/L Mather, an engineering officer, in a full-page hilarious story in the station paper. F/L Mather had been disturbed by word that somebody, unable to get the wheels of his Cessna down, had crashlanded at Mohawk airfield. Complaining noisily that these things always happened in the middle of his smoke period, F/L Mather gathered together a Flying Officer and a Flight Sergeant, and set out in a Cessna to investigate the accident. Enroute, the flight looie wondered loudly "why the damn fool of a pilot didn't use his side crank."

On the Flying Side / 27

Approaching Mohawk, the Flying officer asked the Flight Sergeant if the wheels of their aircraft were down. Advised they were not, the officer, surmising they were stuck, ordered the Flight to crank them down with the side crank.

When that failed, F/L Mather ordered, "Here, give me that damned crank."

After Mather had a go, the Flying Officer asked, "How about it. Have you got them down yet?"

"No, dammit," Mather replied, "we'd better go back and crashland."

We'll let Cunningham's description, in part, give you the rest of the story.

F/S B.: "Will it hurt, sir?"

F/L Mather: "Mentally, yes."

The next scene took place as the aircraft skimmed the Trenton field, "meat wagon" in attendance.

F/L Mather: "Praise the Lord and brace your constitution."

F/O L.: "Well, here goes nothing, hang on."

(Great screeching on the ground, aircraft makes a beautiful crashlanding).

F/O L.: "Get out, Flight, and see what damage has been accomplished."

(All concerned get out of the aircraft and are rushed upon by a throng).

Airman: "What happened, sir?"

F/L Mather: "Get me an engineering officer ... What am I saying? ... By the way, laddie, what time is the next smoke period?"

This incident aside, Maintenance Wing not only did an admirable job of keeping aircraft in good flying condition, it used its skills to convert some aircraft to uses other than for actual flying training.

One that I recall was the Station Hospital ship, a converted all-white Fleet Freighter in which the Fabric Section installed a comfortable upholstered interior.

Another was a Lockheed Hudson on which Maintenance did a terrific job in turning it into a deluxe passenger craft used by officers of the Visiting Flights. Three Hudsons were eventually converted for this purpose — with the first conversion program assigned to F/O Songhurst. Conversion required a major stripping and rebuilding, and fifty-five workers from about a dozen different shops worked on the job at one time or another during the three months spent on the first aircraft. There was such pride of accomplishment that it merited a feature story in the station paper, with photographs of all who worked on the ship.

On the day of the test flight by W/C Terry, OC of CFS, it was arranged for an NCO from the Photographic Section to go aloft

Tiger Moths and Harvards lined up in 1942. The base had about 50 aircraft in 1940 — close to 150 by mid-1944.

One of the Lockheed Hudsons which were converted to deluxe passenger ships for use by FIS Visiting Flights.

Below: Some of the 55 officers, men, and women who completely stripped and rebuilt three Hudsons.

in an Anson to take pictures of the Hudson in the air. I was on that test flight. Just before taking off an officer called toward the hangars for airmen to come aboard and fill up the plane. Running bodies converged on the aircraft from all directions. Every seat was filled and many airmen stood in the aisle. The scene brought back memories of my pre-war days, packed in the old Toronto Yonge Street streetcars during rush hours. Lacking any knowledge of the plane's capacity I wondered if we'd get off the ground but we did — easily.

In the air, everybody was on the lookout for the Anson and its photographer. And every so often somebody would holler out that he'd caught sight of it. This would bring about a surge of bodies to the side of the plane from which the Anson had been spotted, causing our craft to tip about and scare hell out of me, whose flying experience was very limited at the time.

Modifications, conversions and experiments appeared to be ongoing activities on the flying side of Trenton. Although it was supposed to be a bit of a hush-hush subject, one of the more frequently-mentioned planes was a Harvard with a special souped-up engine. It was called "The Jeep" after a character which, I believe, appeared in a late-1930s "Popeye" comic strip. The aircraft, I was told, was not listed on inventory. Because of this, it was flown off to another base prior to any visit to Trenton by the Inspector General — and flown back after he had left our station. One day, somebody came to my office to report that "The Jeep" had flown from Trenton to Toronto — or Toronto to Trenton — in twenty-nine minutes, which was considered very fast in those days, for a Harvard. The person who told about this expected me to write up the feat in CONTACT but somebody else told me to forget about it. The station paper had a wide circulation, with copies going to Ottawa and to a number of civilian newspapers — so I guess bragging about an aircraft which wasn't supposed to exist would have been a dim thing to do.

Of course, there were much faster aircraft at Trenton. We had a Hurricane which the CO and other senior officers would fly. On Sunday, March 12th, 1944, the then CO, G/C Bell-Irving, flew it during a height test to what was believed to be a new record on the station. He took off at 1430 hours and was watched by scores as, with the aid of oxygen, he climbed steadily. He reached a height of 35,000 feet before returning safely to the ground at 1610 hours.

Most of the airmen sent to Trenton's Aircrew Reselection Centre were not only disappointed but bitter. Many had never had a chance to fly so if an opportunity for a flip came along it would be grabbed. One day, I recognized F/O P.S. Naudain, a student instructor, walking along the south station's main drag. Naudain had been on my course at No. 3 ITS, so I asked for a flip. Sure thing.

It was my first. Flying in a Harvard at about 10,000 feet on a beautiful sunny day I was beginning to think there was nothing to this flying business when Naudain, without advising me, decided to show how much he had learned since our days on Course 35. Whether or not this was the accepted way of introducing the uninitiated to aerobatics, I don't know — but I was against it. Back on the ground I paid no thanks to Naudain, being too busy trying to make my way to the nearest hangar washroom.

Most of my other flights in and out of Trenton were routine but one day I was asked to interview F/L Lewis, OC of the Armament Flight, and do a story on dive-and-low-level bombing practices. I decided that if I appeared stupid when things were explained to me (not a great task), I might be invited to go along on a practice to see for myself how things were done. I was.

My pilot was P/O John Rennie, a student instructor. We flew in a Harvard carrying eight bombs under its wings to a bay near Presqu'ile Point, site of the bombing range. Practice consisted of using the first four bombs for dive bombing — which was carried out by diving at an angle of forty-five degrees from a height of 2,000 feet, releasing the bombs at 900 feet, and recovering from the dive at above 500. Performed from four directions, downwind, upwind and two runs acrosswind, the exercise involved certain aerobatics that made it very popular among the student instructors but not with me. After pulling out of the fourth of these dives my face was as green as the verdant fields below. Four low-level attacks followed — after which, since we had finished early, Rennie kindly suggested I might like to fly elsewhere and do some aerobatics. I declined, wondering at the same time if the washroom in the Armament Flight's hangar was in the same place as in the other hangars.

Besides bombing, students at Armament Flight spent several hours at gunnery practice, using both camera gun and machine gun. As was explained to me, the RCAF had little time to train men merely to fly. Fighting was the only thing that would beat the enemy and this was the only type of instruction which equipped men to eventually do the trick. As instructor strength in Canada grew, many of the instructors who trained at Trenton were able to be released for overseas duties — the dream of any man wearing wings.

Like a whirligig increasing its scope as it spins, training of RCAF flying instructors, with Trenton's CFS and FISs as its hub, flung itself ever outward until by December 1942, it was near to fulfilling maximum requirements. The growth and strengthening of these important schools could rightly be called the BCATPs spinal column. The efforts and the results were a credit to all who served in the air and on the ground during the momentous war years.

Musing About the Muse

Canada's largest-ever air show was probably the one held at Trenton on September 12th, 1981, to help mark the 50th Anniversary of the base. In terms of variety, the planes on display from the Canadian forces, the RAF, the U.S. Air Force and civilian organizations ranged from old World War I fighters to the latest in jets. It was exciting just to view the aircraft on the ground and even more so when they took to the air. Yet one of the more memorable events for me, as part of an estimated crowd of 100,000, was the graceful manoeuverings of a glider. As it traced its silent and intricate patterns in the sky, a voice came over the amplifying system reciting the epic poem "High Flight" — apparently a common occurrence at air shows all over the world and at many aviation events. The U.S. astronaut, James Irwin, for example, quotes from the poem in his lectures. Yet few people know anything about the author, John Magee, Jr., and his short but illustrious career, which can be touched on only briefly here.

John Gillespie Magee was born in Shanghai of an English missionary mother and a father who was an American Episcopalian minister. Although most of his education was obtained at a boarding school and the famous Rugby Public School in England, he was attending Avon School near Hartford Connecticut in 1939. There, despite winning a top scholarship to Yale, he grew restless at news of the bombing of England and, in 1940, headed north to join the Royal Canadian Air Force. At Ottawa, sixteen pounds underweight, he was told to return in two weeks, fattened up. By much overeating and avoiding all forms of exercise, he achieved the necessary weight and was accepted as an aircraftsman, second class. Early in 1941, he was at Elementary Flying Training School at St. Catharines, Ontario, where he distinguished himself by soloing after only six hours, when the average was about ten. He later received his wings from Wing Commander W.A. Curtis (later Air Vice Marshal), proceded overseas, trained on Spitfires and, by mid-

October, was on operations — intercepting bombers over the North Sea and Holland. His end came suddenly in December 1941 in a tragic midair collision. He was nineteen. An accomplished poet in his youth he wrote, at age sixteen, "Brave New World", which won a prestigious prize that had also been won thirty-four years before by Rupert Brooke, his idol. Had he lived, Magee might have become one of the foremost poets of WW II.

Is there something about the air force that brings out the poet in young men and women? In the very first mimeographed copies of CONTACT in 1940 there were poems — and the trickle that started in the first printed issue in January 1942 soon became a flood. We sometimes had to chase up news and stories — but never had to ask for poems.

Contributions would be sent to the CONTACT office — most of them signed, but now and then a particularly good unsigned one would arrive. We'd publish most of them, even the unsigned ones — giving credit to Anon. Many poets brought their poems directly to the station paper office where they would stand around awaiting comment — or asking if and when their efforts would appear in print.

Poets at Trenton were not only numerous — many were overly gabby, writing verse after verse without apparent end. In fact, at one point, we inserted a notice in CONTACT under the heading, "Modern Poets Short on Hair but Long on Wind". Part of it read...

"We have no desire to discourage or trample on the aspirations of our bards but wish to point out that poems containing twelve, sixteen or twenty-two verses, such as have been arriving lately, take up far too much space in our small paper."

There were serious and humourous poems. Among the latter which appeared very early in 1942 were contributions from F/O C.W. McLeod. His first was "CFS - She's Heart of Hair Train Plan", followed by "Dat Goddam Bird De Link" and "I'm Post for Oversea". McLeod later teamed up with cartoonist F/O Hugh Rickard to produce a book — the story in which, told in dialect, related the experience of "Joe", an earnest, brave, hardworking French-Canadian airman.

Among the more serious poems was a notable contribution from an unknown author — for he signed his work only with the initials M.J.C. We never did find out what the initials stood for but the poem arrived just as we were preparing our souvenir VE Number. It seemed created especially for the occasion so we made a rare exception by giving it a full page to itself, superimposing the type on a coloured full-page photograph of a Lockheed Electra in flight.

Musing About The Muse / 33

THEY TOO BELONGED TO TRENTON
Who trained here, pausing for a moment
In that wild rush which hurried them
From desk and factory
To battle with the Nazi Vulture
And his Luftwaffe brood.
Keen eyes, restless,
Seeing something far beyond our gaze,
They hurried by,
And even as they paused
Seemed somehow different, apart.
They had to be away
To keep their rendezvous
With darkness.

In darkness did they fight
And in the darkness won.
Through them light comes
For us,
For a world once slave now free,
For all humanity.

The darkness swallowed them,
They came not back.
But darkness cannot hold them.
We shrine them now
Within the light of sacred memories.
The world shall hallow them forever
Heroes of the air.
And we believe
That there beyond the darkness,
Above life's overcast,
They live forever in the light.

—M. J. C.

Another noteworthy unsigned poem which we felt deserved a full page with illustration was called "Airmen's Prayer". I can't recall how we obtained it — but an obituary in a Toronto newspaper in November 1983 disclosed that it was written by the late Wishart Campbell, who was a Flight Lieutenant at Trenton in 1944, and a well-known singer and musician. During the war, the Airmen's Prayer was selected as the official RCAF hymn.

> Pilot Divine, and Lord of all on high,
> Thine are the starry squadrons of the sky,
> Lead us whose wings for freedom's sake now soar,
> Into our hearts Thy faith and courage pour...
> And hear our prayer.
>
> Set Thou our course whose trust is laid in Thee,
> Oh, Thou who chartest all eternity.
> Through cloud and sunshine, through the darkest night,
> Guide Thou our wings who battle for the right...
> And hear our prayer.
>
> Father and Friend, in Whose Almighty Name
> We dedicate our lives to freedom's flame,
> Bless now our wings as on through space we wend,
> Bless us who fly to Thy care our souls commend...
> And hear our prayer.

By mid-1942, the poetry pages were headed by the word "RHYMETIME" in very large type — and a small drawing of an airman in the characteristic pose of somebody reciting. Most poems, serious or amusing, long or short, good or bad, carried some kind of message. One poem might have been called — "Even In The RCAF A Policeman's Lot Is Not A Happy One".

Here is the first of six verses:

> We call him Gestapo, bull and dick,
> We say he simply makes us sick,
> But if we're robbed, we're awfully quick
> To call a Service Policeman.

The poet? Cpl Alred, S.P.

The arrival of airwomen resulted in more poems as the girls took pen in hand and helped swell the flood. Among the early contributors were Sgt M. Morton and AWI Bernice Conrad. The contributions of Conrad were a portent of things to come, for this energetic and dedicated airwoman was soon into everything. She worked for the Service Police and became known as "Connie the Cop". In addition to her poems, she acted as a reporter and columnist for CONTACT, played roles in the station's theatrical shows and participated in umpteen other station activities.

One of the more prolific Trenton poets was LAC Dutton of Central Flying School. A contributor of various types of poems from the very early CONTACT days, he turned his attention to airwomen when they arrived. He was in favour of them — when not everybody was — and his first poem about them, called simply, "The Airwoman", put his side of things across in no uncertain way. We liked his second contribution, "Who is she?"

> Who is she of whom I write?
> Daintier than a woodland sprite,
> With hair, like gold that's fairy spun,
> Impris'ning the glory of the sun,
> With eyes like flowers washed in dew
> Rivalling heaven's clearest blue,
> Whose smile was made to charm all men,
> Calling them back to her again.
>
> I see her now in air force blue,
> Oh, how strange at times it seems,
> Though to me she's unknown, 'tis true,
> All my life I've seen her — In my dreams.
> Who is she?

There was a surprising number of sentimental poems written and published. Some, like Dutton's were about airwomen or women, period, Others, written by WDs, were about men in their lives who were in areas of dangerous operations overseas. While love and tenderness were often evident, the objects of affection were not always human. One guy who had obviously been in action overseas, Waldo MacCausland, became quite sentimental in a long poem titled, "To My Wellington Bomber".

No report on poetry at Trenton would be complete without a few words about "Al Pat" or, using his real name, F/Sgt Alexander Joseph. A First World War vet, it seemed as though Al performed his Second World War duties for the RCAF while writing poetry — not the other way around. His standards were simple — "If it rhymes, it's poetry." He turned out a tremendous number of poems, most of them patriotic — and he compiled some of them into a book which he called, "Rhymes of an Old War Horse". When he left Trenton he was well on his way to a second volume which he planned to call, "BANG! Explosions in Verse by Al Pat". I ran into Al Pat after the war and was not surprised to find him still writing poetry and earning a bit of a living at it — one of the few poets able to do so, I should think. He would solicit donations from firms to help publish his books, most of which found their way into veterans' hospitals. Al never went anywhere without his poems. I once saw him in a march-past of RCAF veterans at a Warriors' Day Parade at Toronto — giving a smart "Eyes Right" at the reviewing stand but with one of his books tucked neatly under one arm.

The late Irish essayist and critic, Robert S. Lynd, wrote: "Indifference to poetry is one of the most conspicuous characteristics of the human race."

Maybe so — but we cared about our poets at Trenton and were happy to make them happy by publishing, most of the time, anything they turned in to the station paper. We classified the contributions under these very general descriptions: (1) Very good; (2) Not bad; (3) Not too good; (4) Unprintable. The democratic system assured that a fair share of each of the first three classifications saw the light of day in CONTACT. Those that were unprintable we returned to their authors as unsuitable — but not before we'd taken them to the Sergeants' Mess where they would be read aloud, just to watch senior NCOs blush.

Another great poet, the American Carl Sandburg, once said, "I've written some poetry I don't understand myself."

We at CONTACT didn't always understand the poems submitted to us — but if publishing them was going to help morale of both poets and readers then, by golly, we were going to do it. And we did.

SWO John Silver as he appeared to tens of thousands of airmen who passed through Trenton

Section Officer H.G. Sparrow, Officer Commanding (right) and A/S/O Ball who headed the newly-arrived Women's Division contingent in 1942.

Vera Charley and Barbara Dye of CFS's Fabric Section paint an aircraft wing.

Harrison Randle cycled his way across Canada entertaining, with his piano playing, at scores of military bases. He is shown here with hospital patients, some of them members of the "Incision Squad".

Home was never like this. Cpl "Moose" Mathews, prominent station fireman and ballplayer, tries threading a needle from his "housewife".

Far right: F/L Jackie Rae, DFC, bothered by the Happy Gang's Bert Pearl, as he tries to entertain at a Victory Loan Concert. Rae is still entertaining today as leader of the well-known Spitfire Band.

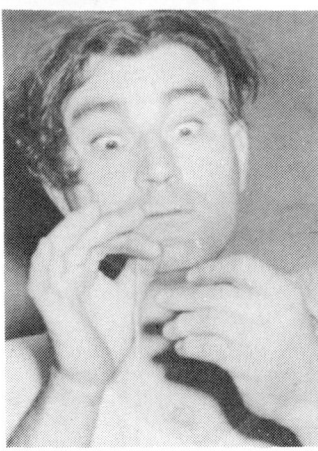

Station Warrant Officer John Silver

Just prior to the 1981 50th Anniversary Homecoming celebrations, I was invited to Trenton to show some of my wartime mementos which included thousands of photographs I wanted to turn over to the base. A young Station Information Officer, Major Lorne Johnson, met me and one of his first questions was, "Did you know Long John Silver?" I knew John very well, of course, but the question surprised me. After all, he was asking about somebody who must have left the base not long after WWII, more than 35 years before. John has become a legend.

Although they may never have met him, almost everybody who went through Trenton during the war years knows of Station Warrant Officer John Silver. Large in size and, when the need arose, large in voice, he was the predominant figure at every parade — be it a regular station parade, a special muster parade, a pay parade or a church parade. Barking orders in a manner that commanded immediate respect and compliance, he would move squadrons and wings of men and women about as easily as most NCOs handled flights. It was rumoured that when he sometimes shouted a command on the south station, airmen would snap to attention at No. 6 Repair Depot a mile north.

There are two stories that cover John Silver's military career. The first, and we'll be brief about it for it does not touch Trenton, is of his service in World War I. Starting as a private in the 96th Lake Superior Regiment, he rose by study and natural ability to become Warrant Officer 1st Class at age 22 — youngest in the Canadian forces. He spent four years and eight months on active service with the Canadian Expeditionary Force and served in Canada, England, France, Belgium and Germany.

In addition to the Service Medal, the Victory Medal and the

Mons Medallion of 1918, he received Honourable Mention in Brigade Orders, represented his battalion at the Duchess of Connaugt Memorial Service in Westminster Abbey, and acted as Corps Sergeant-Major to General Currie when he took the salute from Canadians crossing the Rhine into Bonn, Germany. He was Regimental Sergeant-Major to His Majesty King Edward VIII when he unveiled Canada's War Memorial at Vimy, France in 1936.

An impressive story — yet this proven capable soldier did it all over again when, in October 1940, he enlisted with the RCAF as a lowly AC2. Just 13 months later he became SWO of Canada's greatest air station.

His route was as a Disciplinarian trainee to No. 1 Manning Depot, Toronto, where he gained his first promotion to Acting Corporal. Transferred to Trenton's Disciplinarian Course No. 5 of the Composite Training School, he had to revert to AC2. He completed the course as top-ranking man with a score of 91.5% and the rating "Exceptional". He then joined Trenton Station Headquarters as Acting Sergeant. There then followed a term as Sergeant Major in charge of Discipline in the Composite Training School, Trenton's largest unit, before, on December 18th, 1941, becoming the base's Station Warrant Officer.

During his many years at Trenton, SWO Silver proved to be a good friend of the station paper. Here's an example...

Pay parades at the base were huge and impressive as thousands of men and women lined up inside and outside the Sports Hangar where the money was dispensed. Always on hand was John Silver, loudly making sure that the long queues moved ahead neatly and that individuals marched smartly away from the tables once they had been paid. It was at Pay parades that John first came to the financial rescue of CONTACT. During 1942, copies of the station paper were given away. In 1943, we had to put a price on the copies — five cents at first and later, ten cents.

Sales, in the beginning, were not what they should have been. Cheapskates avoided buying by latching on to their friends' copies. Some genius then decided we should try selling CONTACT at pay parades, while personnel were still clutching their money and before they could reach the wet canteens. Tables of copies of CONTACT were set up at the hangar exit, manned by goodlooking airwomen. As soon as John Silver saw that many airmen were bypassing the girls, still hoarding their pay, he took action. As the men wheeled smartly away from the pay tables, mentally counting their take, John would shout at them — "Get your CONTACTS over there." Knowing the SWO, the men interpreted John's shout not as advice but an order — and the station paper's circulation grew impressively and predictably.

40 / Station Warrant Officer John Silver

It wasn't only at parades that one found John Silver prominent and active. He loved the station, and everything that was happening on it was of great interest to him. I recall reading somewhere that he had been a boxer in his youth and this explains not only his participation as MC at all major fight nights but of his more direct interest in the boxers themselves. He was proud of the station's fine boxing teams and travelled with them when they went off the station to compete. Because of his interest and ability as MC, the boxers considered him part of their team and he appeared in photographs with them in that capacity.

Annual Field Days, now called Air Force Days, would disclose a gentler side of John as he helped in lining up little children for footraces and other events. There is a wonderful photograph of him enthusiastically urging on a determined-looking little girl that demonstrates this side of John's nature much better than I can describe it.

If there was a blood donor clinic, John would be there, not only to help keep things running smoothly but to give blood himself — and he was no longer a young man then.

But parades were his true love — parades of any kind. In June, 1943 he was presented with a Bible by Commanding Officer G/C McBurney — given in appreciation of the Major's expert handling and keen interest in the weekly church parades. Sometimes the church parades were compulsory and the resultant large attendance needed the skill of John to keep it properly organized. When church parades were not compulsory, John would still be there. On his way to the Astra Theatre, where Protestant services were held, he would sometimes stop an airman walking in the opposite direction and, with his authoritative manner, shame him into joining him in going to "church". I know this from firsthand experience.

The two Trenton bands, brass and trumpet, were favourites with John mainly, I suppose, because of their involvement with parades. Usually, at the completion of a weekly or any other important parade, the bands were used to lead the march past the saluting base, where they would wheel off and come to a halt to the east of the Admin. Building's main doors. There, they would continue playing until the many flights of men and women on the large parade square had left it.

Some time in 1944, nostalgia for the infantry route marches of the First Great War must have swept over the SWO for he arranged for the Headquarters flights to go on such marches — though very short in comparison to the 1914-1918 ones. Instead of marching along the many roads of the station, the band would head out the main gate and proceed east along the two-lane, Highway No. 2, followed, of course, by the Headquarters flights. What this did to traffic on Highway No. 2 and to the

Station Warrant Officer John Silver / 41

tempers of civilian drivers is left to your imagination. Traffic problems were the least of John Silver's worries, however. To further simulate the route marches of World War I, John would urge us to sing whenever the band stopped playing. So we'd tramp along, shouting out the words of "Roll Out The Barrel" from our World War II repertoire, and "It's A Long Way To Tipperary" from the songs of World War I. When we had proceeded far enough to suit John — and too far to suit us — he would call a halt and dismiss us to the side of the highway, where cigarettes would be lit. Very authentic infantry stuff.

There weren't many of these marches. When they were discontinued, we presumed the Department of Highways had requested that the RCAF get the hell back on its base.

Perhaps the most important day at Trenton for John Silver was Wednesday, June 14th, 1944. There was a parade, of course — a very big one. This time John not only set it up but was one of the main reasons for it. Eight distinguished commissioned officers and SWO Silver were being honoured by His Majesty for outstanding service and devotion to duty. The awards included an O.B.E., an M.B.E., four Air Force Crosses, two Commendation Certificates and an Operational Wing.

The M.B.E. (officer of the military division of the Order of the British Empire) belonged to SWO John Silver. It was presented to him by the Station's Commanding Officer, G/C A.D. Bell-Irving. I never saw John look more proud. Nor has there been, in my view, an RCAF Warrant Officer more deserving of the honour.

Something New in Blue

September 10th of 1942 brought about a situation which many a Trenton diehard airman swore just could not happen. Airwomen made their appearance on the base.

Arriving from the railway depot by bus, the main body of girls was met by the station band which led them in a march-past in front of the Administration Building where W/C F.C. Carling-Kelly, acting for Air Commodore F.S. McGill, CO, took the salute and later said a few words of welcome. The welcome did not end with the march-past however, for that evening a special dance was held in the Sports Hangar.

While this was taking place, airmen who for weeks before had discussed with horror the intrusion by women into their domain, stood looking on with disapproval while some wondered audibly what the RCAF was coming to. Others, not so concerned with tradition recognized that the coming of airwomen would give a tremendous boost to the station's social activities and literally — and later, actually — welcomed the WDs with open arms.

Greeted, then, by a mixed reception of cheers and misgivings, airwomen made their first entrance into the station life at Trenton. With a month's basic training behind them, they arrived looking a good deal smarter than had been anticipated and their keenness on parade was soon noticed by officers and discips, who passed their impressions on to the other-ranks.

"The women," they claimed, "are making you look terrible," a comment which did nothing to increase the women's popularity.

Officer Commanding the first contingent of WDs was Section Officer H.G. Sparrow, ably assisted by Assistant Section Officer Ball and Sgt Norma H. Reany. Reminiscing about the good old days later on, S/O Sparrow was always ready to take issue with SWO John Silver over his statement that "Those first WDs were a frightened looking lot."

"No more frightened than WO1 Silver," she would argue, pointing out that even A/C McGill was concerned over the arrival of the airwomen.

The CO was, too. I well recall his consternation. Determined that the approaching arrival of women foreboded nothing but trouble, he called for a full station parade at which all officers and men were warned that the first person stepping beyond the bounds of decency with the arriving WDs would be clamped down on hard and fast. "And you all know what I mean," the CO added belligerently. In short, nobody was to look at any of the arriving young airwomen as an assigned, official or legitimate "Target for tonight". The parade was dismissed with mutterings from all concerned.

"We didn't want the women in the first place," was the prevailing mood. Some young men adopted an air of innocence and declared they couldn't for the world understand what the CO had been talking about — and later turned up among the first of very few who actually did step beyond the bounds of decency.

Those in authority stepped warily those first few months and rules pertaining to "out of bounds" areas for airmen and airwomen were strictly enforced. For instance, airwomen making their way to the guardhouse had to stay on the main road. No cutting corners by taking the road up past the tennis courts, behind the airmen's barracks. Others whose work took them to the old KTS building or anywhere at the southern section of the base could not cut off behind No. 1 Mess Building but had to take the main road to the Admin. Building and turn there. Service policemen were constantly patrolling the areas around the WD barrack blocks. A blinding searchlight was played over the front-door entrance to the airwomen's barracks and it became necessary for an airman to say goodnight to his evening's companion in its glare. Sensitive at first to this exposure, airmen (and airwomen) soon got used to it and farewells, while cut short by the presence of service police, were soon conducted in a normal over-amourous manner.

In the meantime, the airwomen were settling down admirably into their jobs. Their strength, at first, included clerks, equipment assistants, telephone operators, meteorologists, postal clerks, cooks, messwomen and fabric workers — some of whom later took courses to qualify as air frame mechanics, dental assistants, motor transport drivers, etc. The wisdom behind RCAF posters urging women to enlist "That Men May Fly" was being ably demonstrated.

The appearance of airwomen at station dances proved to be most welcome for not only did they provide an answer to the shortage of feminine partners, they instituted new ideas in decoration and design that added much in furnishing a more pleasant atmosphere.

Furnishings were not confined to the dance areas. Some of the NCOs started to put drapes over the windows of the Sergeants' Mess. Initial entry of women NCOs into the Mess resulted in a sharp drop in the amount of profanity there. The drapes brought it back up again. Old veterans of the first world war,

Trenton's own Rondelles Concert Party, 1942. Left to right: AW1s Edith Motley, Bettie Lynnes and Ella May White, Sgt Fran Dowie, LAC Mike Betts, AW1s Nonie Stockdon and Mary Gary, and Cpl "Bub" Saunders.

Nobody cast slurs at Kitchener, Ontario with this quartet around. All from the same town and all teletype operators, from left to right are: LAW Kay Lederman, Cpl Pat Mullins, and LAWs Joy Brandow and Bette de Roit.

Trenton's spit and polish reputation was boosted in 1942 by this award-winning KTS precision drill squad.

Hi jinks! These men of the visiting USAAF Band were former members of the Les Brown, Tommy Dorsey and Glen Miller orchestras.

Extreme right: Aboard the Empress of Canada when it was sunk 500 miles off the African coast, W/C F.R. Edmund survived to become Trenton's SAO in 1944.

serving again in the second, suffered most. Sulking in corners and bent over beerstained cribbage boards, they emitted tortured mutterings that failed completely to dissuade the women from prettying the place up. Some of the younger men helped put up the drapes, bringing about a split in the male ranks that livened things up no end.

The first social event arranged for women on the base was the first day's evening dance in the Sports Hangar. In spite of the muttered male protest against women in the forces, this event brought out a record number of airmen including, it was thought, a fair number of AWOLs. It was probably the first time since the beginning of the war that the entire station strength was all present and accounted for.

More such dances resulted in some of the first dates being made between airmen and airwomen — and many a humble AC2 from then on found himself in the unique situation of kissing his corporal "Goodnight" ... and liking it. It represented a sharp break from tradition.

In spite of the CO's fears, it didn't take long for the women to become an accepted part of camp life and the effect was good all around. Without even an inspection in the offing, airmen were polishing buttons and boots, and conditions had relaxed to the point where the women were permitted to wear civilian clothes in off-duty hours and brightly coloured dresses at station dances.

While the latter trend brought a welcome change from the monotony of blue and khaki it brought with it, as well, certain disadvantages. Without a uniform, it was impossible to tell an officer from an other-rank and many an airman found himself in the embarrassing position of having to salute, some morning, the very woman he'd whistled at, yoo-hooed at or held too closely the night before.

Daytimes saw the range of the airwomen's work increasing. Pictures of some would appear in the station paper, showing them washing down aircraft, packing parachutes, working in the meteorological and photographic sections, doing just about every job previously done by men.

There was no stopping that first contingent of airwomen. They had a job to do in the air force and they meant to do it. And if the reward for a hard day's work was a program of recreation then they, too, meant to obtain their share of that.

By early 1943 they were into everything. Baseball, for instance, had long been a form of exercise in which many airmen took part — but ball games soon became not much more than a male spectator sport. Women formed their own teams, wore snappy uniforms and outdrew the men's games by several score to one, it being the opinion of most that while women also could play a lousy game of ball they looked much better than men while doing it.

As recreational facilities increased, WDs grabbed their share. One became vice commodore of the airmen's yacht club, they became members of the miniature rifle club, they formed some fine basketball and bowling teams, muscled in on use of the indoor swimming pool, claimed their share of time on the tennis courts. There was hardly a sport or recreation in which they were not participants.

The muscling in on use of the indoor swimming pool resulted in an interesting incident. Announcement that there would be mixed swimming at the pool brought out a tremendous number of participating airmen — so many, in fact, that women who turned up became unnerved at the sight and decided to forego the first evening's swimming. They disappeared. This brought about a decision to cancel the mixed swimming program for that evening and allow the lads to cavort in the water as nature intended them to do and which they had often done before — that is, sans clothing. A few minutes after the men had the pool to themselves, Section Officer Marj Looker arrived for a dip. Not having been informed of cancellation of mixed swimming she trotted nonchalantly into the pool. So long, nonchalance! The WD officer's dash from the pool set a record for speed at the base which, I should think, still stands.

While work and play went on, love inevitably bloomed. On April 9th, 1943, a four-month romance culminated in the first all-Air Force wedding being held at Trenton. LAW Mildred R. Assels of Winnipeg became the bride of LAC Howard Ross of Windsor, N.S. Other airmen-airwomen weddings followed and in May 1944, the Officers' Mess was the setting for the marriage of Nursing Sister Esther Miller to Flight Lieutenant Glen Maynard.

Mention of nursing sisters is a reminder of one of the sports highlights that took place on the base — the official opening of a new outdoor swimming pool in one corner of the sports field. One of the featured events was a relay race between a team of nursing sisters and one of airwomen. The first airwoman had gained a slight lead when the second airwoman, clad in a two-piece swimsuit, dived into the pool. As she struck the water, two portions of her swimsuit whose job it was to meet at the back, parted company — thereby causing the contestant, a Sgt Murphy, to come to the surface clutching desperately at the upper portion of her anatomy. A wave of silence swept over the crowd, then, realizing what had happened, the predominantly male audience roared its approval as the sergeant struggled to reach the edge of the pool while still trying to cover her embarrassment. This event pretty much assured successful attendance by airmen at all future swim competitions and exemplified the kind of thing which made our war different from the old one.

Something New in Blue / 47

In overcoming the early resentment of men to women in the forces, the airwomen at Trenton covered a lot of ground in a very short time. Every now and then, civilian newspapers would publish photographs of air force girls climbing in and out of motors, with daubs of grease on their cheeks and foreheads, the implication being that airwomen were a tough bunch, devoid of femininity. Did the girls get up in arms over this? No — the airmen did, with a number from Trenton writing letters and articles to set the record straight.

Three years at Trenton saw some remarkable changes take place in the Women's Division and while many airmen were skeptical of the benefits of airwomen prior to their arrival there were none that I know who felt that way at war's end.

The New CONTACT

In an article entitled "Goodbye Now", in the December 1942 CONTACT, it was explained that an Air Force ruling prohibiting the sale of advertising had forced the station paper, "like all good things, to come to an end."

No more CONTACTS! To those of us who had worked on the magazine and to thousands of airmen and airwomen who enjoyed reading their free copies, it was a bitter disappointment. Yet, in retrospect, killing the old CONTACT because of lack of advertising revenue was one of the better things that happened at Trenton.

Early in 1943, it was decided the station needed a CONTACT in some form. With no advertising revenue to count on, an Advisory Committee under F/O D.B. Harvie had to find new funds. It was decided that a price of five cents a copy would have to be charged for any new paper. When it was found that this type of revenue would be insufficient to meet printing and publishing costs, the Commanding Officer, G/C R.E. McBurney, approved a suggestion whereby the balance would be met by the Station Central Fund, in addition to substantial contributions from the Officers' and Sergeants' Mess Funds.

The new publication was to be a "newsy" tabloid sort of paper, less elaborate and smaller (sixteen pages) than the old one because of the tight budget. The old publication had been printed on slick paper, was thick in pages, and featured large photographs. "Classy" would be a good description of it. We didn't think so in 1942 but when compared with the new 1943 CONTACT, another description which could have been used was — "staid".

A policy was set up for the new publication. It was to be an "Airmen's Paper" (and an airwomen's, of course, for all those ex-WDs who read this and have become liberated). Through the new paper, personnel were invited to submit criticisms and suggestions — things the old paper never encouraged.

ACI Stan Helleur, the former CONTACT editor, had been lifted from Trenton to help start the national publication, WINGS, in Ottawa. A new editor had to be found. I had been art editor of the old magazine but when I found Helleur with more work than he could handle — and me with not enough — I tried to help out by writing. I even had a few bylines.

This was good enough for the new CONTACT Committee.

"Sargent," they said, "you're the new editor."

When I explained that I was not an experienced editor I was told I would be given help. It arrived in the form of AC1 Ed Hayes of KTS, a young experienced journalist who had worked with the Kitchener Daily Record. Several other ex-journalists were discovered in the ranks of the Reselection Centre. These old hands at writing didn't mind working for me. They could write — but some couldn't put the paper together. I could.

For the first few issues I let myself be guided by this experienced crew which I found, later on, was akin to a lamb letting itself be led to the slaughter.

One of the first persons to respond to the invitation to submit criticism was a character who signed his too-long letter with the non-de-plume, "Aussie".

"Aussie" didn't like the station laundry system and my helpers went to his aid by placing a large heading over his front-page letter — "Poor Laundry System Exposed", followed by the subheading, "Writer Tells How Airmen Victimized".

On an inside page, there was another two-column heading which shouted — "Airmen and Mess Officials Clash on Butter Situation". One column, containing beefs from the airmen, carried the subheading — "Poor System, Boys Contend". The "boys" contended that rationed butter wasn't being distributed fairly. Several were quoted in the story.

The heading over the second column read — "Fail To Use Heads, Is Reply" ... this being the start of a rebuttal by Section Officer H.J. Scharff of No. 1 Airmen's Mess, and F/Sgt E.A. Bedard, chief cook at the Mess.

Another story with a two-column heading claimed — "Airmen's Wrath Raised As Sandwich Jumps To A Dime". Sandwiches in the canteens had been selling for a nickel.

Canteens, dry and wet, were in an uproar when CONTACT came out. Airmen and airwomen waved their copies in great glee as they shouted and argued with one another. Never had the station paper been so popular with the masses. I was the only unhappy person.

"I'm in trouble," I thought. The paper had, in effect, backed and fueled what appeared to be several mutinies.

I had never met the CO but expected to shortly. However, nothing happened. G/C McBurney and his appointed CONTACT Committee had, in their wisdom, apparently considered pages of the station paper as an appropriate place to let off steam.

Nevertheless, I took firmer control of the paper and permitted only one more outrageous heading — "Rent Ad Causes Storm of Protest by Airmen". The complaint told how landlords in the

Placed on the staff of the station magazine in late 1941, the author, F/Sgt Bill Sargent, became editor of CONTACT in early 1943.

From left to right are: F/O T.W. Spear and S/O M. Looker, two members of CONTACT committees during 1943 and 1944, Cpl Alex Lebskin, assistant editor, and Sgt Lorraine McGavin, WD editor.

These airwomen boosted circulation — of the station paper, of course — at Trenton's massive pay parades. Back row, left to right: Terry Schuss, Gladys Moore, Anne Morrison and Wynne Thompson. Front row: Gora Dotter, Lorraine Davenport, Jeanne Stinson, Lois Rathwell and Barbara Gibbons.

town of Trenton allegedly discriminated against airmen in their advertisements in the Trenton Courier-Advocate. I figured it was all right to pick on civilians.

Other signs that the new CONTACT was going to be a paper for all airmen/airwomen was the deluge of contributions of news that flooded the office. In the old CONTACT there had been a half-page column called "Trenton Topics" in which some promotions were recorded, leaves reported, and the odd bit of harmless gossip included. In the new paper, every section of the station's south side and every flight on the flying side was given space to publish its own news.

A lot of the gossipy news may have already been known to personnel before it was published — but reading about F/Sgt So-and-So's fling with Cpl Betty What's-Her-Name behind Six Hangar in CONTACT was more fun than learning about it by ear. While news of promotions, leaves and gossip was sometimes interspersed with extra spicy items, only rarely was it necessary to do a little editing.

Jokes were introduced in 1943. I can't recall that we ever printed a joke in the very proper 1942 CONTACTS but we used lots of them in the new magazine. They were very popular, so much so that after a while we had to devote a whole page to them under the heading of "Just Plane Nonsense", while using still more as fillers throughout the paper. Sometimes I'd be asked how we acquired so many jokes. Some were obtained from the U.S. Camp Newspaper Service which included them in monthly clip sheets to editors of base newspapers. Others, I lifted — or adapted is a better and truer explanation. Almost any joke about civilians can be changed into a service joke by changing the characters in it into service people. Sometimes we would get a laugh at the office when we'd see such jokes printed in civilian papers — with credit given to CONTACT.

Here's one joke we ran which had us wondering whether it would encourage or discourage potential WD recruits...

A comely young lady had enlisted and her friends were bidding her a fond farewell. "Be sure to write to us often," said one of them.

"I will try," was the answer, "but judging from my first few days' experience, I am going to be very busy saying, 'Yes, ma'am' all day and 'No, sir,' all night."

When starting up a new publication, one might imagine that the first issue would be a predominantly staff-written one. Not so with the new CONTACT. When word that we were restarting the station paper got around, we received such a flood of contributions we had to print a notice in the very first issue that we couldn't possibly use all submitted material — a good indication of what a service publication can mean to armed forces personnel.

52 / The New CONTACT

Some Flight and Section reporters, starting at the top and from left to right: LAW L.M. Rathwell, F/L R.K. Cameron, Cpl F.P. Switzer, Cpl R.M. Vandrick. Second row: Sgt S. Samuel, Sgt K.B. Scrimger, F/S M.A. Ryan, Cpl W.A. Hume. Third row: LAC H.J. Smith, LAC A. Gould, WO1 S. Zadco, Sgt F.E. East. Fourth row: F/S A. V. Levack, Sgt A.J. Pianosi, LAW M.T. Howitt, LAW G. Dottor. Fifth row: Sgt W.C. Hibbert, Cpl J.M. Soutter, Cpl H.W. Lawrence, LAC R.F. Madill.

Anne Morrison became editor of the new WD page in 1943, and some other contributors of interesting stories were Ivan Stumpf, Betty Roche, Connie the Cop, of course, A.L. Gould, Ron Rewbury, C. Lees and Irv Johns.

Even after the turmoil created by Letters to the Editors carried in the first 1943 issue, we continued to publish others. Many contained suggestions or outright beefs about something or other — but we never aided or abetted any of the causes, leaving the letters to speak for themselves. There was a very serious NCO, Sgt Wolman, who could be counted on for a letter now and then but he never confined himself to Trenton or RCAF topics. Instead, he concentrated on such weighty subjects as "Winning the Peace". CONTACT was his soapbox.

The new paper was selling well and we were able to increase the price to ten cents a copy without a murmur of protest. Some credit was given to a team of airwomen, selected for their winning ways, who would set up shop at pay parades held in the Sports Hangar. Their efforts themselves made news. One airman complained — "Trying to get out of the Sports Hangar without buying a CONTACT is like trying to blast Gibraltar with a peashooter." Another airman, more intelligent, claimed that by buying three copies he got a date for himself thrown in.

Command at Trenton changed hands in December '43 with G/C Bell-Irving taking over from G/C McBurney. Funds were found to reintroduce coloured covers and more pages were added. Whether the price increase to ten cents a copy made these improvements possible — or whether the new CO tapped the till of the Station Central Fund for a little more money I don't know ... but colour certainly spruced up the paper and the extra pages made it possible for us to use more from the overabundance of submitted stories, poems and cartoons.

Changes in the masthead were taking place in 1943 and 1944. President of the CONTACT Committee when the paper was restarted with the March '43 issue was F/O D.W. Harvie who remained in the post until September of that year when F/L R. Davidson and F/O S. Tooke took over as an Advisory Committee. These were followed by F/O T.W. Spear, F/L J. McGrail and S/O M. Looker. CONTACT was fortunate in the CO's selection of these officers for all were helpful and supportive. None imposed his or her view as to the paper's content although two or three wrote editorials now and then.

One officer used to come to the office and ask what we intended to feature in the next issue. If he felt something more exciting was needed he would pace about, muttering...

"If only somebody would drop a bomb on the parade square."

This wish was repeated several times so I'm pretty sure who the officer was — but today ex-F/L Bob Davidson claims he can't recall getting that worked up about things.

Other masthead changes included LAC A. Lebskin who became almost a full-time staff member, AW1 Lorraine McGavin who took over as WD editor, Sgt J. Pianosi, a PTI who became Sports Editor, and Photographers Cpl H.L. Woodward and Cpl J.M. Soutter.

While, after our first experience, we no longer went out of our way to back readers' complaints about the base, the paper did, on its own, campaign against increases in the price of pressing uniforms at the station press shop. Today, we think of inflation as something that started in the early '70s and is now only beginning to subside in the '80s but inflation was rampant at RCAF Trenton in the '40s. A 1943 story is interesting.

In 1942, the station press shop charged a dime to press trousers and tunic. Later in the summer, the price was raised to fifteen cents — a nickel for trousers and a dime for tunic. In mid-1943, the price was raised again and here, in part, is how the station paper reacted:

"Complaints have been rife since the station press shop increased its fee from fifteen cents to twenty-five cents — and Trenton town firms from twenty-five cents to thirty-five cents.

"Prices were raised shortly before summer dress went into effect. This aroused the airmen's ire to a greater degree, particularly in view of the fact that summer uniforms must be cleaned and pressed more often than 'blues'."

We lost that fight.

In 1944, CONTACT's circulation had almost doubled from the year before. There were growing signs of the paper's popularity on the base, off of it in Canada, and overseas. Station personnel were sending copies home to families or elsewhere to friends. On many occasions, whole training courses took out subscriptions upon graduating. WO1 "Pat" Cousins, warrant officer in charge of the Motor Transport Section, arranged for the purchase of subscriptions for all his lads posted overseas.

Letters telling of the paper's popularity outside Trenton were arriving regularly. Flight Officer J. Wright, formerly in charge of WDs at the base, got carried away and wrote — "I get more news from CONTACT than I get from the Ottawa Journal." Sgt Archie Pierce, formerly of Headquarters, wrote that his station in England was under the command of Air Commodore McBurney and that the former Trenton CO was surrounded by a staff that appeared to have been lifted intact from Trenton. Names mentioned were F/O John Collyer, F/Sgt Al Rodgers, Sgt Stew Foster, Cpl Gayneau and Cpl Sharpe. "You should see them grab for CONTACT when it arrives," Pierce wrote. From France came a message from F/O Stan Helleur that former Trentonians there "are anxious for the station paper."

The New CONTACT / 55

As the war drew to a close, RCAF publications began to fall by the wayside. WINGS, the national publication produced by Headquarters in Ottawa, was unceremoniously closed in December 1944 while its editor, F/Sgt Ed Hayes, was on assignment in Vancouver. The final edition of WINGS ABROAD, official chronicle of RCAF activities overseas, rolled off the presses in London, England in June 1945.

Trenton's CONTACT continued publishing blessed, in one way, by not being dependent on government funds for its existence. However, shortly after my discharge came through in October 1945, CONTACT did cease publication ... to arise no more until the late 1960s. It is still going strong today.

On the Waterfront

Trenton's waterfront was a busy place during the war years — with activities galore on the water from spring through to fall, and inside the Seaplane Hangar during the winters. Activities were varied but fell, most of the time, under two categories: (1) The work of the Marine Section; (2) The play of the aeroquatic clubs.

I'm not sure when the Marine Section was first established on the base but on my arrival in the fall of 1941 it was an important and going concern. In addition to serving as a school for Motor Boat Crewmen (as a unit of KTS) it had its own fleet of marine craft and acted, as well, as a host to many others. A lot of the ships in the Seaplane Hangar during the winters found their way there from Bombing & Gunnery Schools of No. 1 Training Command, after ice conditions had curtailed their activities on those bases. Some of them came in convoy from as far as 250 miles away, their crews bringing them each November through the Great Lakes and Welland Canal to Trenton. Used at B&G stations mainly to patrol the ranges and warn other craft away from danger, they also patrolled waters adjacent to flying fields, where their jobs were to race, with their crews, to the search and rescue of airmen forced down onto lakes.

Trenton not only had its own fleet for these purposes but it also served as the winter maintenance base where our men would scrape down the hulls of B&G boats, repaint and varnish them. This work was done inside the hangar but every boat was quickly placed outside after completion in order to prevent dryness from opening up its seams. So there were marine craft on the waterfront all year around. During work on the hulls of the boats, engines were taken out and sent to No. 6 Repair Depot where men, dispatched from the Marine Section, worked on them.

F/O A.J. Maddox was OC of the Marine Section when I arrived but he was eventually followed by F/L Schwab. A warrant officer who served under both of these men, and who was very helpful in establishing the recreational yacht clubs, was WO2 J.E. Hebert.

Several types of marine craft were used by the RCAF, some built especially for specific purposes, others — sleek looking motor yachts donated by citizens and still others chartered for the duration.

Preparing the boats so they would be ready for use each spring kept men of the Marine Section so busy they would often work on weekends.

According to a story in the station paper, some of the men developed an uncanny ability at finding jobs that just had to be done when the Sunday morning church services were about to begin. SWO John Silver brooded about this.

One Saturday, he entered a wet canteen and found a number of seamen lubricating their vocal chords and engaged in loud singing. So impressed with the quality of the voices, was the SWO, that he told the group their talent deserved a better setting — and mentioned, as an example, the following day's church service. The SWO could also be heard to mutter something about repercussions, etc.

The next morning found the front seats of the church service occupied by almost the entire staff of the Marine Section, with F/O Schwab included in the group. As they lent their voices to the hymn singing, Sgt Major Silver stood to one side, smiling benevolently — while F/L Padre Nimmo looked down from his improvised pulpit in astonishment.

The Marine Section people were a skilled lot and could, and did, make a number of boats. Some boats, though, were too big for the facilities but even though many had to be built elsewhere in civilian shipyards, they often ended up at Trenton for finishing touches. In the fall of 1944, for example, three new patrol boats built in Orillia, Ontario for use on the Atlantic coast, arrived at our base for wireless installation.

One innovation of the Marine Section was a combination sleigh and boat. The first of its kind, it was made for use in rescuing aircrew whose planes had crashed through ice or into water where ice had to be crossed to reach them. Built on the lines of a flat-bottomed barge, it had handles at each end and was equipped with large steel runners underneath. The runners were attached so the boat could be pushed across ice to open water or run up from open water onto ice.

There were often boats of another kind on the waterfront — flying boats and seaplanes. Some were attached to the base while others were visitors. A Fleet Fawn used to appear early each spring and be taken up for trial flips by officers from CFS and Maintenance Wing. One impressive-looking all-white flying boat was the station's hospital ship. A Grummond Goose, used by high-ranking officers from AFHQ for reaching seaplane bases, turned up now and then. Personnel were sometimes startled by the sight of a Walrus aircraft, belonging to the Kingston Fleet Air Arm, which sometimes set down at our base. A pusher type of plane with an 850 h.p. Pegasus engine and a four-bladed propeller, it was one of the Navy's oldest types and, in the opinion of Trentonians, the oddest. Yet while Trentonians viewed the plane with bemused interest other Walruses were being looked upon by dozens of ditched WWII airmen with an effection usually reserved for guardian angels. Slow and poorly defended, Walruses had a remarkable ability to land and take off in waves several feet high and they built an enviable record in air/sea rescue. That the aircraft flew at all surprised many people — yet it shouldn't have, for its designer was R.J. Mitchell, a railway engineer turned aviation engineer who is better remembered for the Spitfire.

During summertimes the motor launches were joined by yachts and sailboats and the waterfront would look like a miniature Newport. Officers had the first yachts, the flagship of which was called the "Astra". In mid-1943, G/C McBurney, CO, who had long toyed with the idea, arranged for formation of an airmen's and airwomen's yacht club. The club's fleet, at first, was to consist of five rowboats, five canoes and four Comet class sailboats. However, there were shortages of everything in wartime. Wood, required for the building of the fleet by the Marine Section, took longer than anticipated to arrive. An Aeroquatic Club had been formed with F/Sgt Phillips as president and F/L Bob Davidson as commodore. When the wood arrived in November 1943, men of the Marine Section soon went to work.

By spring 1944, all the boats were finished and enthusiasm among would-be sailors was high. On May 24th, the official launching ceremonies took place with the then CO, G/C Bell-Irving and his wife in attendance. Mrs. Bell-Irving launched the first boat and Mrs. R. Davidson the second. Three other sailboats were launched by airwomen — one by a Bermudian, one by a Canadian and the third by an American. There was a small rental fee for boats which was later dropped — but full membership in the Aeroquatic Club, with all privileges and advantages, cost a whole dollar a year.

With yachts, sailboats, rowboats and canoes all in use, there was a sort of romantic air about the waterfront. In fact, one airman, quoted in CONTACT, pointed out that the station "does everything except provide the moon." Sometimes the base was even able to provide that — but it wasn't always necessary.

One day, the commodore of the Aeroquatic Club came into my office and asked that I publish a story about how the CO had rescued an airman and airwoman whose sailboat had become becalmed on the Bay of Quinte. The CO had seen the sailboat from his house, gone down to the waterfront, commandeered a motor launch, reached the sailboat and towed it, with its occupants, to shore. I promised to look into the story. Trenton

Typical summer scenes on the waterfront. Above is F/L Schwabb, OC, Marine Section, testing a sailboat's rigging.

At the right, from top to bottom are shown:

A Fleet Fawn landing on the bay.

Cpl Beals gets ready to tie up a rescue craft as Sgt McCrea issues instructions.

PTIs are shown crossing a stream on ropes during Commando Course lesson on Baker's Island.

This interesting craft, thought to be the first of its kind for use in rescuing downed airmen, was designed to cross ice into open water or to move out of open water on to ice.

was a very crowded base. There were not many places where a man and woman could make love in private. The couple in the sailboat thought they had found such a place. They didn't want to be rescued but as the airman explained to me — "What are you going to do when the CO throws you a towline?"

There were other attractions along the waterfront — sometimes quite unexpected ones. The winter of 1943-44 was unusual in that the Bay of Quinte had frozen deep from one end to the other, giving the base one of the finest sheets of ice anywhere. Oldtimers in the town of Trenton claimed it was the first time in 20 years that the Bay had not been covered with snow. One could skate for miles in any direction. Some airmen did, in fact, go down to the waterfront, put on skates and skate into Trenton town to see a movie — then return the same way later on. A new source of enjoyment for Canadian airmen was to go down to the Bay and watch RAF lads trying to learn to skate. LACs Bill Scott and Archie Currie of the Marine Section scrounged materials and made an iceboat — and took their speedy craft for some thrilling spins. The appearance of other iceboats a mile or so offshore indicated that the townspeople were also being innovative.

In the summertime, turtles were another source of interest and enjoyment along the waterfront. There were so many turtles at Trenton during the war years that it was once suggested they should be made part of the establishment. The station paper carried a number of stories about the size of some of the catches made — with some men bragging of picking up turtles that were two feet in diameter while others told of scooping up tiny ones not much larger than a twenty-five-cent piece. One story told of an airman who had been bitten by a turtle — but his mates said the turtle had been unduly provoked.

On Baker's Island, we once looked over a cliff and saw scores of turtles of all sizes on the shore. Startled at our approach, they scrambled into the Bay and bobbed about in the water about 40 feet offshore — waiting for us to depart and leave them to do whatever turtles do when gathered in such large numbers.

Airwomen loved the turtles. One airwomen found a turtle making its way across the sports field. She picked it up and took it to the WD barracks where it became a much admired and overfed pet. The ease with which the turtle slipped into this envied position astounded some airmen — a few of whom used to spend their spare time lolling about outside the WD barracks, trying to figure out ways to get inside.

Readers who remember the wartime waterfront would be amazed at the place today. Gone are the rescue launches — replaced, I suppose, by helicopters on the flying field. Across the water in front of Baker's Island is a fleet of pleasure craft and yachts that would be the envy of many civilian yacht clubs. But the biggest surprise would be Baker's Island itself which is now reached by a wide causeway, turning the place into a sort of peninsular jutting out from the land base. A road circles the now cultivated island and at one spot, from where I saw the scores of turtles in 1945, there is a beautiful yacht clubhouse, complete with kitchen, bar, dance floor, etc. Airmen of the '40s who had to traverse the rugged island's tough commando course would find it a pleasurable cakewalk today.

Four Commanding Officers

From the time war in Europe broke out in September 1939 until hostilities in the Pacific ended with Japan's surrender at Singapore on September 12th six years later, Trenton Air Station had six distinguished commanding officers. They were (with ranks shown at the time of takeovers): W/C C.M. McEwen, W/C J.A. Sully, G/C T.A. Lawrence, G/C F.S. McGill, G/C R.E. McBurney and G/C A.D. Bell-Irving.

I served under the last four, three of whom were veteran First World War fliers, the other a young permanent force officer. At the outbreak of war, W/C C.M. McEwen had been commanding RCAF Trenton for almost a year and was a Group Captain when he left the base in early 1940. This officer is better known by thousands who served overseas as A/V/M "Black Mike" McEwen, AOC of No. 6 Bomber Group based in Yorkshire. McEwen was replaced as CO at Trenton by W/C J.A. Sully who had served as second in command at the base until he took over full command in the spring of 1940. Sully's term at Trenton was during the period when the Station was experiencing a building boom.

Most of us who served on Canadian air stations during WWII had little contact with commanding officers, especially if we were on large bases such as Trenton and were in the NCO or other-ranks category. Our views of these men were usually from afar, such as on station parades. Not much was known of their backgrounds except by those who happened to be on a base when a change of command took place. On those occasions, a short biography of the new CO would be published in the station paper. As a member of Trenton's CONTACT staff, I read and proofread stories on the first three of the commanding officers I served under — and wrote the fourth myself. So I learned more about the service lives of these men than might have been possible had I been in other work. The first of my commanding officers was...

TRENTON'S SIX WARTIME COMMANDING OFFICERS

Air Vice Marshal C.M. McEwen

Air Vice Marshal J.A. Sully

Air Vice Marshal T.A. Lawrence

Air Vice Marshal F.S. McGill

Air Vice Marshal R.E. McBurney

Air Commodore A.D. Bell-Irving

G/C T.A. Lawrence

Sometime in 1982, while twiddling the dial on my TV set, my attention was caught by a National Film Board presentation of some of the RCAF's pre-war activities. The elderly officer being interviewed was Air Vice Marshal Lawrence and his comments were interspersed every so often by film clips showing him in his much younger days as a Canadian Air Force pioneer. I sat up and took notice for there, on the screen, were views of some of the events I'd only read about, briefly, forty years before, when Lawrence had taken command at Trenton. He was, the films showed, in command of air operations for a 1928 expedition photographing and making visual reconnaissance of ice conditions of the Hudson Strait, prior to the opening of the Northwest Passage to Fort Churchill.

G/C Lawrence was born in 1895 and educated in schools at Barrie, Ontario. Like a lot of other young Canadians he entered the Canadian army during the First World War, enlisting in the 76th battalion in 1915 and reaching England, then France in 1916.

Near the end of 1917 he made a move which, in later years, was to prove so valuable to the RCAF. He responded to the call of the Royal Flying Corps for Canadians with an urge to fly, as did a number of other soon-to-be-famous young Canucks. By Christmas he was back in England, learning the rudiments of flying. In 1918 he received a commission with the RAF and returned to France with the 24th Fighter Squadron in September.

Discharged at the end of the war, Lawrence was back in Simcoe County in 1919. His love of flying and the proximity of Barrie to Camp Borden proved too much of an attraction and by February 1920 he was back in the air, working hard for the Canadian Air Board.

At Borden and at Ottawa, he was tagged as a man who could be given a job and left alone with it. The photographic and reconnaissance expedition he commanded was, for example, based in the great snowy barrens of the north for sixteen months, visited only once a year by the government ship *Nascopie*.

During this assignment he, F/Sgt Duncan Black, and the port

manager for Revellon Freres, were forced down by a blizzard that snowed them in so deeply, and iced the engine so badly, that it took two full days of hard shovelling and "cooking" to make the ship serviceable enough to fly out. On another occasion, there was a seven-week trip by sleigh, with an Eskimo and his dogs, from Port Burwell around Ungava Bay to Wakeham, sleeping in snow huts and "eating God knows what."

Lawrence was back to the warmer climes of Borden in 1930 and 1931, with No. 2 Training Squadron. Subsequent service saw him as Liaison Officer with the RAF at the Air Ministry in London ... a participant in the first experimental Air Mail flights in a Fairchild 31 from Halifax to St. John over a foggy Bay of Fundy ... on a course in Army Cooperation at Old Salum near Salisbury, England ... then duty again at Borden, Rockcliffe and Trenton.

When the Munich crisis captured headlines in 1939, Lawrence was at Halifax, engaged in the quiet work of preparation for the war to come. He became Director of Air Staff Duties and, later, Director of Plans and Operations at Headquarters. There, organization of the Air Defense of Canada was the job on hand. Lawrence and his staff drew up the plans for Canada's great wartime system of coastal defense by air.

Group Captain Lawrence arrived to take command at Trenton in November 1940, when the station was half the size it was when he left in March 1942, just sixteen months later. Among his many contributions to station life was authorization for construction of the Airmen's Mess Building and formation of CONTACT magazine.

G/C F.S. McGill

While it is true that most other-ranks seldom met their CO at Trenton, a few that did were responsible for G/C McGill becoming known as "28-day McGill" not long after he took command of the base in March 1942. These were alleged miscreants who had found themselves up on charge before the CO — pleaded guilty or were proved guilty — and had received sentences which seldom varied, that is, twenty-eight days in the "Digger".

At time went by, G/C McGill earned a reputation as a tough but fair and square commanding officer who became popular with all ranks. Officers and NCOs at Trenton during McGill's days will remember him for his hilarious stories, told in French-Canadian dialect, at various Mess events.

Telling the story of G/C McGill's flying career is much the same as telling the story of the air force in Canada for, comparatively speaking, they grew up together. Born on June 20th, 1893, McGill was one of the first Canadian youths to pursue aviation to a practical extent. Graduating from McGill University, he became interested in the Royal Naval Air Service and, after learning to fly at Ithaca, N.Y., obtained the Aero Club of America's license No. 30 for float planes. He then journeyed to London, England where the RNAS welcomed him.

During the second year of the First World War he suffered a broken arm in a crash into the Thames estuary. Upon recovery he went to Navigation School and followed this with a spell at the Naval Gunners' School at Whale Island. Then came a brief period for Lt McGill with the famous Dover Patrol, later becoming second in command of the First Mobile Squadron off the Scilly Islands.

The end of World War I found Frank McGill in the United States as an advisor and test pilot on twin-engined flying boats but before settling down to civilian life he spent most of 1919 back in the Scilly Islands. Most of his postwar time was taken up with executive duties with Dominion Oilcloth and Linoleum Co., and he became one of Canada's outstanding athletes and, later, sports organizers.

A Canadian title swimmer and captain of a Dominion championship water polo club, Frank McGill starred on senior football and hockey teams. He helped organize the Montreal Light Aeroplane Club and formed the 115 Fighter Squadron of Montreal for the Auxiliary RCAF.

When war was declared again in 1939, McGill became a wing commander with the RCAF and three months later was named Commanding Officer at Camp Borden. Then followed organizational work at Ottawa Uplands, a spell at HDQTS as Director of Postings and Records and, when organization was needed on the East Coast, he was the man who whipped things into shape there.

In April 1942, Trenton Air Station welcomed him as its Commanding Officer. Full station parades were regular features each Thursday during the war years but the one on August 6, 1942, had special significance. G/C McGill had been promoted and it was at this parade that he took his first salute as Air Commodore. To my knowledge, no other officer attained this rank while serving as CO of the base.

During his tenure at Trenton, airwomen arrived to work at the station. Apprehensive, at first, about their arrival, the CO soon changed his mind. In a farewell message, he wrote — "Yes, the girls have proved a great asset, not only during working hours but in helping make our dances, entertainments and athletics more enjoyable for all."

G/C R.E. McBurney

When Group Captain McBurney took over command from A/C McGill in January, 1943 at the age of thirty-seven, reaction among the other-ranks was mixed.

"Too young," claimed a number of airmen who had become used to First World War fliers as their COs. A let's-wait-and-see attitude was prevalent.

Not so among the airwomen. They were all for a younger CO — and particularly liked the fact that this one was "so good-looking." I brought up the subject of Trenton's wartime COs at a recent WD reunion and found that ex-airwomen, now in their 60s, still remember G/C McBurney for, among other attributes, his good looks.

G/C McBurney was born August 17, 1906 in Montreal but, with his parents, moved while an infant to Saskatoon. There, during his boyhood, he set two goals in life — one to become an electrical engineer, the other to fly.

He accomplished his goal of becoming an electrical engineer through study, from 1923 on, at the Universities of Saskatchewan and Manitoba — acquiring his degree in 1930. During these years he pursued his other objective.

In 1923, the air force introduced an expansion plan under which university students would receive flying training during summer months. Young Ralph McBurney became eligible in the first year and in May, 1924, he reported to Camp Borden as a provisional pilot officer. For the ensuing three summers McBurney trained at Borden, winning his coveted wings in 1926.

Granted a non-permanent commission, he remained at Borden for the winter, taking an advanced flying course — then was sent to Jericho Beach, B.C. where he trained on seaplanes. Subsequently, he was posted to Winnipeg Air Station where his first big responsible job was that of supervising construction of a detached operational base at Snake Island.

In August, P/O McBurney was transferred to Ladder Lake, Sask., to assist in fighting a fire hazard. Enroute, he became lost due to a pall of heavy smoke, rain and a faulty map. Forced down in the Deshaumbault Lake sector, he and his mechanic wandered about for six days. They were finally discovered by an Indian who paddled the pilot officer about sixty miles to Pelican

Narrows, a fur trading post near the Churchill River.

Resuming his university studies in the fall, P/O McBurney returned to Lake Winnipeg in the spring as Officer Commanding the detachment. One of his jobs was to take the fire ranger to scenes of conflagration, and mercy flights involving trappers and others were numerous.

In 1930, he became a Flight Lieutenant. The following year he was placed in charge of a crew of photographers and surveyors whose job was to make photographic strip maps to provide aerial pathways in the western provinces and the Northwest Territories.

Following service included a course in army cooperation at Old Sarum, England, a term in Winnipeg, then eventual posting in 1933 to Camp Borden as instructor in the newly-formed RCAF army school of instruction. In 1935, he took the Signals Officers' Course in England. Back in Canada the following year as "Adviser Signals" at AFHQ, he became a squadron leader, then returned to England to attend the RAF Staff College. The outbreak of war brought about his recall to Canada as Director of Signals. Promoted to Wing Commander in 1940 and Group Captain in '41, he became Trenton's CO in January 1943.

During his ten-month tenure, G/C McBurney was a staunch supporter of the station paper, resurrecting it in March 1943 after it had ceased publication in December '42. He was responsible for starting up a number of new facilities, among which were two that were probably unique in the RCAF, i.e. officers' and airmens' yacht clubs. He left Trenton to take command of RAF Station Dishforth, England, in No. 6 (RCAF) Bomber Group.

G/C A.D. Bell-Irving

G/C Bell-Irving's term as CO was the longest of the wartime COs — twenty-three months — and because of this he became better known by more personnel. He took command in November 1943, retiring in September 1945.

Born in Vancouver on August 28, 1894, Allan Duncan Bell-Irving attended school in Scotland and was on his way home from there when war broke out in 1918. One of his first acts back in Vancouver was to enlist as a private in the 16th Battalion, thus becoming one of six Bell-Irving brothers to see service in the First World War. One was killed and all six decorated.

Overseas, he was commissioned and served with the famed Gordon Highlanders. Later, in France, a fascination for flying grew strong and, in August 1915, he was seconded to the Royal Flying Corps. He trained as an observer when flying's main function was to report enemy troop concentrations and movements. It was while on reconnaissance that Bell-Irving was first wounded and shot down. Convalescing in England, his enthusiasm unimpaired by his recent misfortune, he studied flying and became a fighter pilot in May, 1915.

Fighting then was often a matter of teaming up with one or two chums and going out to fight the enemy in individual encounters. When the machine gun was first introduced as part of an aircraft's armament, observers would still take along rifles that hitherto had been their only form of protection or attack. Pot shots would be taken at the enemy in an effort to lure them close enough to get in a good machine gun burst.

It was while flying with Albert Ball, a celebrated English ace, that Bell-Irving was once more wounded and shot down. His days as a fighter pilot over, he was invalided back to England where, on his recovery, he became Chief Flying Instructor at the Gosport School of Flying. At Gosport, misfortune again overtook Bell-Irving. While testing an experimental aircraft that just wouldn't fly, he crashed and was badly injured. Quite lame, and requiring the use of two crutches to get around, he later took command at Gosport before returning to Canada in 1918.

For his exploits in the air he was awarded the Military Cross and Bar by the British and decorated with the Croix de Guerre by the French.

In civilian life, Bell-Irving maintained his interest in flying and started the first auxiliary squadron in Vancouver. When the club became an auxiliary squadron of the RCAF, he stayed on as wing commander. At the outbreak of war he became a staff member of Western Air Command, joined the staff of No. 1 Training Command in September 1941, then became CO of No. 1 Bomb and Gunnery School, Jarvis, Ontario in July, 1942. On November 4, 1943, he took over command at Trenton.

Interested in making the off-duty lives of personnel more comfortable, he built the popular Wintergarden and a new outdoor swimming pool for airmen and airwomen. He was a well-known visitor to the waterfront where he delighted in his favourite sport of sailing.

*   *   *

A/C Bell-Irving died a number of years ago, according to a nephew, British Columbia's recently retired Lieutenant Governor, who says, "We all miss him a lot." A/V/M McGill died at the age of 86 in June, 1980. Active in community projects, he served as chairman of the advisory board of the Montreal General Hospital from 1972 right up until his death there. In a photograph taken during a COs Reunion at Trenton in 1981, A/V/M Lawrence appears healthy and happy, as does A/V/M McBurney. At the time of writing, Lawrence, at 88, was living in Toronto where he keeps busy writing his memoirs. A/V/M McBurney resides in Ottawa where he is working on plans to record memories of RCAF bush pilots — what they did, how they lived, what the aircraft were like to fly, and so on. Also, he is cooperating with the Western Canada Aviation Museum in Winnipeg by providing information of heritage interest about opening up of the north by air.

Pin-Ups and Cover Girls

Although every serviceman in World War II had his favourite pin-up girl it was generally agreed that Betty Grable, the Hollywood actress known as "the girl with the million dollar legs", held down top spot. Lloyd's of London had actually insured the legs for $1,250,000. The most popular pin-up picture of the actress was a rear view showing her dressed in a white swimsuit, and peeking saucily over her shoulder at the viewer. American Armed Forces distributed 2,000,000 copies of this photograph to their troops — and millions more reached Allied armed forces through pages of newspapers and magazines.

It was to the shame of Trenton's station paper that it did not get around to publishing a photograph of the forces' favourite pin-up girl until November 1943. Even then, it showed only a one-column, front view of the actress in the role of "Sweet Rosie O'Grady" from a film of that name — not the universally famous picture.

While we were a bit slow off the mark at CONTACT we made up for it later on. In March, 1944 we turned the back cover of the magazine over to a pin-up for the first time. Our girl was Ginger Rogers — in a very revealing (for those days) pose. We made the picture serve a double purpose — entertainment and instructional. Under it, in big type, was the question — "What Do You Plan To Do With Your Spare Time?" ... and the subheading, "This question is in no way connected with the above illustration but nevertheless should command your attention." We then suggested the using of spare time to prepare for civilian life — by taking some of the Canadian Legion's educational courses. Some airmen complained that diverting attention away from the pin-up was a dirty trick — so we never did anything like that again.

Some of the other Hollywood stars we featured as pin-ups were Dolores Moran, Alexis Smith (now a star in "Dallas"), Virginia Christine, Joan Leslie, July Bishop, Brenda Marshal and Rita Hayworth. The photograph of Miss Hayworth was a dandy. Taken from above, it showed the glamourous redhead lying on a background of satin as though she were sunning herself on a beach. Part of the caption read: "We hope this new portrait will satisfy the insistent clamourings of the wolves not only at Trenton but at all other areas where Canadians are in training or battle action."

To me, one of the most amazing examples of the publicity agency business at its pushiness took place at Trenton on April 13th, 1944. A publicity director from a film company, accompanied by photographers from No. 1 Training Command, arrived at the station and informed all and sundry that Belita, a reputedly beautiful, talented twenty-year-old skater and dancer, had been chosen PIN-UP GIRL of RCAF Station, Trenton. I was told to gather a group of airmen as an audience so I ducked into the offices of the Administration Building and rounded up a dozen volunteers. Cameras then flashed as a huge picture of Belita was unrolled and my volunteers gathered around to gaze admiringly at the girl they could now call their own. Two days later, newspapers all across Canada proclaimed her the pin-up girl of RCAF, Trenton.

"Who is she?" airmen asked. "Belita who?" they wanted to know. "Has anybody heard of her before?" they queried one another.

Lots of questions but no satisfactory answers. The young English actress may have been well-known in Britain or Europe but nobody at Trenton — nor many people in Canada, it seemed — knew of her. Yet here she was, chosen, the reports claimed, by men at Canada's largest air base.

CONTACT dutifully reported this event — omitting the fact that the airmen who had supposedly selected this pin-up were clueless as to who she was.

On going to press with the May issue, we ran a STOP THE PRESS item advising readers that a wire had been received from Belita expressing her delight at having been picked as Trenton's official British Pin-Up Girl and promising that she would make our station "one of my stops on my next tour of Army camps." Army camps?

Belita never did turn up at Trenton and, to my knowledge, no films featuring our official pin-up girl appeared at the station's two movie houses.

Pin-up pictures developed along quite new and unexpected lines in September 1944. That month marked the second anniversary of the arrival of airwomen at Trenton so CONTACT not only featured a well-illustrated story on the WDs but used the full back cover to show a photograph of an airwoman. The featured WD was Cpl Lorraine McGavin, a PTI and Women's Editor on the station paper. She was shown in a head and shoulders shot, a partial profile, in full uniform against a background of an RCAF flag. The very fine photograph was by Sgt J. Burnett of the base Photographic Section.

We intended to revert to another Hollywood glamour girl for

LAW Sees and LAC Evans

Sgt McGavin

LAW Vaughan

Cpl Jay

LAWs Higginbottom and Stark

LAW Davenport

LAW Neville

LAW Keens

Shown above are some of the airwomen who appeared as cover girls during 1944 and 1945.

Although few knew who she was, Belita, a skater and dancer was named Trenton's official British Pin-up Girl. Airmen admiring her photograph are: F.D. Snider, A.H. Greenwell, K.B. Scrimger, C.E. Vallance, J.O.E. Proudier, E. Couilliard, R. McTaggart, J.W. Singleton, G. Woolford, H.L. Phelps and T. Venney.

our next issue but the Commanding Officer, G/C Bell-Irving, had other ideas. He liked the WD photograph and ordered that from then on the back cover of CONTACT feature an airwoman. While this upset our plans, it suited nicely a number of airwomen who had continually badgered us with the query — "What have they got that we haven't got?" ... referring to the Hollywood stars. A provocative question.

It dawned on us at CONTACT that the CO hadn't stipulated that airwomen featured on our back covers had to be in uniform — so we decided that the next one wouldn't be. Airwoman Subject No. 2 literally fell into our hands. Unbelievably, we hit the jackpot. A photograph arrived at our office of LAW Jane Vaughan, a lovely looking Trenton equipment assistant who had recently been crowned No. 1 Training Command Backstroke Swimming Champion. She was shown in a one-piece swimsuit against a background of the officers' pool — leaning, slightly, against the pool's ladder. Nothing any better, with the possible exception of the Rita Hayworth picture, had appeared in the numerous submissions of film star photographs sent to us by aggressive movie publicity agents. We felt great about it and even submitted graciously to the "We told you so" taunts of airwomen when LAW Vaughan appeared on the back cover of the October 1944 CONTACT.

There followed a succession of CONTACT WD pin-up girls or cover girls, as they then became known — all very attractive young ladies. Among those from the Station staff were LAWs Ginger Adams, Kathy Sees, Shirley Keane and Lorraine Davenport.

At the beginning of this period we discovered that we, as selector of cover girls, had suddenly acquired a new importance among airwomen. Some who had previously been disrespectful on occasion began to flatter us unashamedly. It was fun but only for a little while. We could use only one back cover photograph a month, so some of the many unsuccessful applicants were soon being disrespectful again. Even some of the nice ones became cool.

It was a no-win situation — so I soon turned the job of choosing cover girls over to others.

After No. 1 Air Command was based at Trenton in early 1945 and the staff began taking an active part in off-duty activities, it was decided to feature some Command airwomen on the back covers. We wanted no part in selecting the girls so the choice was left to Cpl McInnes, who submitted a column of Command news to the paper each month. He decided to hold a contest in which twenty-two airwomen were nominated as cover girls — an indication of the interest in this monthly CONTACT feature. Two airwomen were eventually chosen — LAWs Teddy Higginbottom and Madeline Stark — and both appeared in attractive blouses and shorts as cyclists. They were followed in months afterwards by Cpl Olive Jay (in uniform for a VE Day shot), LAWs Duffie Neville and "Pat" Patterson, and Cpl Millie Livingstone.

When the practice of featuring airwomen as cover girls was started some airmen bemoaned the fact they were being deprived of pictures of glamourous Hollywood movie stars. There were, however, no complaints as time went on. There were some very pretty airwomen in the RCAF and Trenton had its share.

Cpl Rene Kulbach, a service policeman and noted Canadian muralist, lent his fine talents to the beautification of the station.

The top mural was in the Wintergarden. The Viking-type mural was part of a larger one at the library's entrance and the bottom one was in the Sergeant's Mess. The top mural still exists at the base. In the picture showing Kulbach seated, he is producing an illustration for a story on the town of Trenton.

Cpl. Rene Kulbach — Muralist Extraordinary

Eyes popped incredulously when members of Trenton's Sergeants' Mess wandered into their dining room in early 1944 and saw a painting which filled almost the entire east-end wall. Some of the lads took one look at the centaurs, half-man and half-horse characters famous in Greek mythology, and swore off any future patronage of the bar. Others sat openmouthed trying to interpret the story behind the painting.

The huge mural became a favourite topic of conversation during mealtimes. We sought out the artist, Cpl Rene Kulbach of the Service Police. Kulbach explained that his work could be called "The Procession of the Goddess of Plenty" — indicated by a golden carriage loaded with fruit and vegetables, and carrying the Goddess. Some of the other Greek mythological characters in the painting were "Bacchus, God of Wine and Merriment, astride a donkey (great for the Sergeants' Mess), and "Pan, God of the Marshes and Friend of the Wild Creatures."

This was the first of several murals painted at the base by the talented Corporal. One, which interpreted the story of North America from prehistoric times to Confederation, covered the walls of the stairways leading up to the Library above the Airmen's Mess. Another, which depicted the wild and woolly west, showed Indians attacking a covered wagon. This mural, full of exciting action, was painted on a very large wall in the popular Wintergarden section of the Sports Hangar. It is still there, today.

Some of Kulbach's work done before the war still exists in civilian buildings. Over the past forty-five years, millions of persons must have gazed upward to admire the beautiful murals on the massive ceiling of the Crystal Ballroom in Toronto's Royal York Hotel. A friend who often attends meetings there claims to have spent a colossal amount of time studying the graceful swans and women when he should have been paying attention to speakers. Another fine Kulbach mural, painted around 1948, graces a large wall in a waiting room of DVA's spacious Sunnybrook Hospital. This one covers 132 square feet and presents a study of Canadian wildlife in pictorial form.

With the exception of a few days, Kulbach's painting in the Sergeants' Mess was done in his spare time, which accounted for the fact that it took almost five months to complete. Each day, after painting, he would carefully conceal his work with sheets, which added to the curiosity of the NCOs. This practice was discarded when later murals were painted and I can recall the interest which thousands of men and women showed as they watched the huge Wintergarden mural take form.

When the skill of the noted muralist was recognized, he was permitted to work full-time on his paintings. The Wintergarden mural was completed in three weeks. For a while, he was posted to Camp Borden where he worked on murals in the Officers' Mess.

Cpl Kulbach was born in Russia in 1908 and lived the greater part of his life until his Trenton days in the Crimea, at the Black Sea. After the Russian revolution, he lived in Germany for three years and Estonia for five — before coming to Canada in 1928. He was a self-taught painter who traced his interest in art back to the time he was five years old and started drawing animals, his favourite subject. Much of his experience was gained by sketching in the Zoological Gardens in Stuttgart, Frankfurt-on-Main and Hamburg. In Canada he traveled extensively — harvesting, fruit picking, cowpunching, painting and sketching until, in 1936, he established a studio in Toronto. There, he became one of the well-known colony of writers and artists living and working on Granville Street.

Before Cpl Kulbach was discharged from the RCAF at Trenton in late 1945, he illustrated a story in the station paper about the town of Trenton — showing the lumbering industry of the 1800s and the little-known-about motion picture industry in the town during the early 1900s. He also produced the beautiful full-page illustration in CONTACT's VE Day Number which depicted the part the station played in achieving victory over the Axis powers. I've often wondered why the illustration was never enlarged and framed and placed in a prominent spot on the base. I recently mentioned this to a base officer and I believe something is to be done about the matter.

Fluent in Russian, German and English, Rene Kulbach was a big, quiet but friendly person. After the war, we stayed in touch for a while. His interest, besides painting, was hunting. It was hard to buy a car in the mid-1940s because few, if any, had been made during the war years — but I had succeeded in getting an

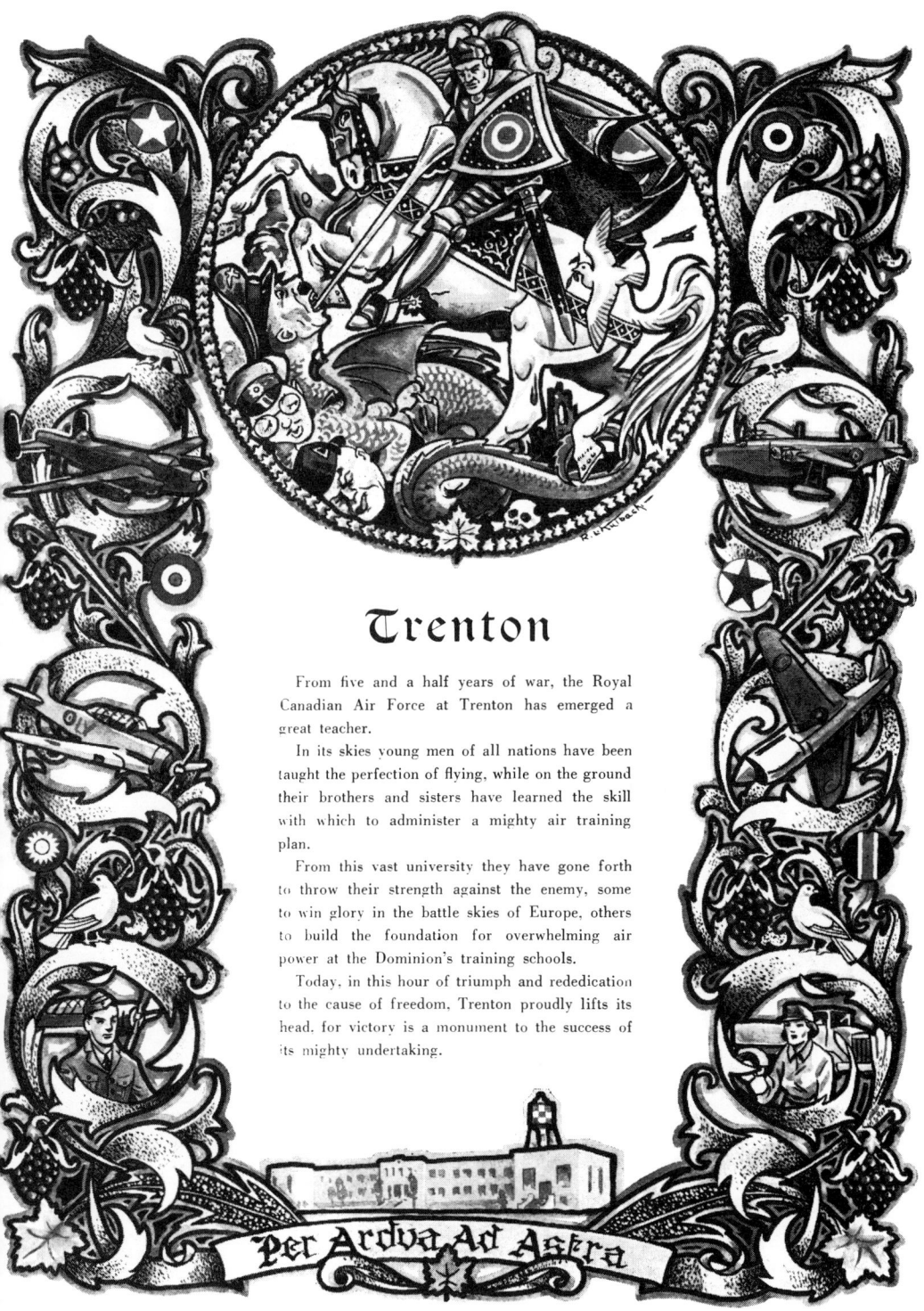

This is an interesting illustration by Cpl Kulbach produced to commemorate VE Day. At the top it depicts slaying of the Axis enemies. Sketches around the side show planes and personnel, a salute to Trenton's participation in the victory.

old, used one. One day, Rene talked me into driving him, his wife and brother to Halton County in Ontario for the opening of the pheasant season. We tramped the fields all day and saw not one bird — but Kulbach was a crack shot and he bagged several rabbits.

While trying to establish ourselves in civilian life after the war in different kinds of work, we drifted apart. It saddened me to read in the 1950s that Rene Kulbach had died. Fortunately his work lives on — at Trenton and elsewhere.

The International Scene

If it was variety in uniform or language you were looking for in Canada, the place to park yourself was in the KTS Orderly Room. Through that section, at one time or another, passed all the men from Aircrew Squadron up for reselection. They represented several Commonwealth countries, the U.S.A. and air forces of a number of European countries that had been overrun by the Axis powers.

Another good view could be had from the large parade square in front of the Admin. Building, during regular station parades. If you were with Headquarters you were in flights that, usually, were first on the square. Then came flights from the flying field, marched across by the station brass or trumpet band. And then, very quietly at first, you could hear a single side drummer in the distance, beating out the step for long flights of KTS Aircrew Reselection and Training Squadrons, leaving their own southern assembly area. As the drumbeat grew louder, you would watch for the first ranks of these flights to appear from behind the Admin. Building. And when they did appear, especially in years leading up to 1943, you quite often saw at the head of the column a half-a-dozen or more men in naval uniform. These were sailors from the Royal Navy's Fleet Air Arm taking their rightful place, as members of the senior service, at the head of the KTS parade. As the flights marched on to the main square you would see other uniforms that were definitely not RCAF, and the game would be to guess what countries they represented.

One afternoon, a member of the station photographic section visited the KTS parade area and took an interesting shot of a group of ten Aircrew Reselection men which, in recent years, has been published in a number of journals. The ten represented nine different branches of Allied air power. Two of the men, in uniforms that made them look more like officers than other-ranks, were members of General DeGaulle's Free French Forces. Other members of the group were representatives of the Czechoslovakian Air Force, the Polish Air Force, RAAF, the Royal Marines, RNZAF, the U.S.A. and the RNZ Fleet Air Arm.

A few years ago I sent a copy of the photograph to AIRFORCE magazine in Ottawa, which published it in its March 1980 issue. It drew requests for prints from a number of former airmen in Canada and the U.S.A. and one, specifically, from a member of the French Air Ministry in Paris. This person was compiling a history of the Free French Air Force. He had been to Canada a year earlier searching for information and photographs of Free Frenchmen who had gone through the BCATP. Some information had been obtained but no photographs. Yet there was AIRFORCE showing a Trenton photograph that included not just one Free Frenchman but two. AIRFORCE sent the request for a print to me. Because of the records in CONTACT, I was able to provide the French Air Ministry official with not only a photograph but information, as well, about where the two men had been based in France, England and Canada prior to their arrival at Trenton.

While the group photograph gives a fine example of the international touch that was at Trenton, it does not represent all countries that had men and women training there. Often, there were aircrew and groundcrew from the Royal Norwegian Air Force, the Free Belgian Air Force, the Netherlands and many other forces. There were Cubans and Chileans, for example, taking training in 1943.

In addition to working in administration and training units these foreign men and women participated in many station social activities — and not just sports. They could be counted on to help with concerts and theatrical shows. In early 1943, citing just one instance, a New Zealander, LAC W.R.A. Raper, carried off first prize in a station amateur show.

Prior to Pearl Harbour, many Americans were on the base, some as instructors and others as grounded aircrew going through the Aircrew Reselection Centre. Most seemed to be aircrew. Often, they made up major portions of training classes and they would chide Canadians with remarks that our force should be renamed the Royal Texas Air Force or the Royal Virginian Air Force. Many serving in Canada (CONTACT's early editor, for example) transferred to the U.S.A.A.F. after their country entered the war. Canada had gained tremendously from their efforts, especially during the early part of the war when instructors in Canada were scarce and the Americans came north to help out in that capacity.

While it is easy to understand the keenness of the foreign chaps in their desire to move overseas into action against the enemy that had overrun their homelands, one would not have expected them to participate very aggressively in campaigns to sell Canadian Victory Bonds — but they did. During the Fourth Campaign, the station paper ran a photograph of five, from different countries, proudly displaying their bonds.

Language and accents, as well as uniforms, pointed up the international scene. Sometimes men from the same European countries would sit together in canteens and messes and converse in their own language adding, in a small way, to a sort of cosmopolitan air about the base. Aussies and New Zealanders lent their distinguishing accents to the mix. It was the Aussies who continued the singing of "Waltzing Matilda" in canteens long after the rest of us had petered out — for only they seemed to know the many verses of this popular song. Contrary to the belief of many of us, "Waltzing Matilda" was quite an old song. It was written during the first Great War by a New South Welshman, Barton (Banjo) Paterson, a war correspondent who scribbled the words on the back of an envelope while in a little bush pub.

The international scene was also evident when soccer, not a notably Canadian game, took over some areas of the sports field. Teams, composed mostly of British players, would visit the RAF base at Picton and other bases to play matches. Rugger was also played at the base in 1942 with teams again made up mostly of Commonwealth chaps.

Lusty voices calling, "Well played, sir," were heard from the sports field in 1941 and '42, and again in 1945, as Britishers, Aussies and New Zealanders brought cricket to the station. Matches were arranged between base RCAF and RAF teams, as well as with other armed forces bases and civilian clubs. One batsman of a base team, playing against a Peterborough team in 1945, was G/C Bell-Irving, the CO.

Men from all over the world came to Canada to learn to fly and fight. To see them at Trenton, at work and play, gave one a clear conception of the outstanding work our country was doing in administering and operating the British Commonwealth Air Training Plan.

In this famous photograph are ten members from the Aircrew Reselection Centre. They represent the following nine branches of Allied air power: Czechoslovakian Air Force, Free French Air Force, Polish Air Force, RAAF, Royal Marines, Fleet Air Arm, a U.S. member of the RCAF, RNZAF and RNZ Fleet Air Arm.

Another example of international participation (right) shows Victory Bond purchasers from Belgium, Chile, U.K., Netherlands and U.S.A.

SWO Silver, MC at most boxing shows, is shown with boxers: Cpl Reschamps, AC1 McPeake, Cpl Miller, Sgt Fulton, LAC Moss and Cpl Blanchard. At right is the genial "Happy Slapper", Sgt Hub Smith.

Fight Nights

News about the sport of boxing is conspicuous by its absence in the CONTACT of the 1980s. Every issue now contains something about karate, which most of us had never heard of in the '40s. Nary a word about official fisticuffs.

This is strange and one wonders when the change took place at which boxing gave way to the Japanese system of self-defense. During the war years there was an abundance of good fighters among men at Trenton. Some old ex-airmen may tell you that there were some pretty good fighters among the airwomen, too, but they are remembering unofficial bouts which do not belong in the telling of this story.

Boxing — or fighting with the fists — is an ancient sport. The Greeks and Romans practiced it at gladiatorial spectacles. It is interesting that, even that far back, they did not use the naked fist. They wore a kind of glove, not to make the blows softer as is the case today, but to make them harder. The gloves were sometimes loaded with iron and lead, which made them terrible weapons, and the fights frequently proved fatal. Later, a mixture of boxing and wrestling became popular but the rules of this type of fighting were revised after several contestants were killed. It was in England, several centuries later (the 18th to be exact) that the "noble art" as it is sometimes called, attained a high state of proficiency and was carried on under more humane rules. From then on, boxing increased in popularity and, at one time, all classes of society took part. There were famous characters of the ring in the 18th century, just as there have been in the 20th, but the most extraordinary was a fighter named Bendigo, who became a revivalist preacher, and of whom the story is told that he once used threats of a pugilistic nature to induce his congregation to give liberally to the collection.

Although we had a padre who sometimes put on the gloves, nothing like that ever happened at Trenton. But a lot of interesting fights took place. And as already stated, our guys were good.

Here are a few headlines from the station paper about fights involving teams from other bases, air force and army.

Undefeated in Five Bouts ... Station Boxers are Victorious ... Local Boxers Win Dominion Recognition ... Trenton Fighters Take Command Titles ... Local Lads Good at Mitt Show.

Not all the fights took place at Trenton, of course. Our station team would travel to Kingston to do battle with the Army — to Picton, Mountainview, Camp Borden and other Air and Army bases. Fights for Command Titles were sometimes held in Toronto. Many of the fight nights at Trenton were held to aid good causes, like kicking off Victory Bond Drives. The team went to Montreal once to participate in a Victory Bond Fight Show being held in the Forum, where the late Lt Jack Dempsey of the U.S. Coast Guard acted as referee for one of the bouts. Trenton's boxers, on one occasion, travelled to Verdun, Quebec to take part in a Czechoslovakian War Relief Boxing Show.

There were always good crowds at the boxing shows — and always, in the centre of the ring, acting as MC and announcing each fight, would be the imposing figure of Station Warrant Officer John Silver, with microphone in hand. Not that John ever needed the amplifying system to make himself heard.

In the March, 1942 issue, a CONTACT writer gave his impression of the crowds. "They were there," he wrote, "for various reasons. Some because they were broke and had nowhere else to go; others were curious because they had never seen a boxing show; others were unbelievers who went only to see how bad it would be, and last but not least, those who would rather swap leather than eat."

Who were some of those who would rather swap leather than eat? We can name only a fraction of the large number but among the more prominent was Sgt Jerry "Smoky" Blanchard, a former Canadian bantamweight champion. Then there was Bob Fulton, who did much to teach and promote boxing at Trenton. And heavyweight Jerry McPeake who, at one time in his station career, scored eight consecutive first-round knockouts, something of a record. Tom Sullivan, LAC Kennedy, Gaston Reschamps, George Tessier, LAC Moss and A.C. Ross are others who come to mind. Then of course, there was "Hub" Smith.

Smitty was a regular on the station boxing team when I arrived in late 1941 and he was still going strong, winning most of his fights, as the war drew to a close in 1945. Hub and his twin brother were only seven when, known as the Cough Drop Twins, they made their debut in the world of fisticuffs. That was back in 1927. Hub was twenty-three and already a veteran in professional ringcraft when I first learned of his skill in 1942. In its March issue of that year, the station paper reported:

"Through the years, from the Cough Drops' first appearance until the Canadian Olympic trials finals in 1936, Hub had a total of 127 amateur bouts, losing only thirteen — and losing in the Olympic trials finals to a fighter later ranked as one of the best lightweights in the world.

"In 1937, Hub turned pro and after two years of barnstorming in the southern U.S., he fought forty-three professional bouts, losing only four. Then came the war and Hub enlisted in the RCAF. Aside from doing his part in the

Motor Transport Section at Trenton, Hub has had fifteen bouts, losing only one to a former lightweight champion from England."

I saw him lose only once during the time I reached the base and left in October 1945. Hub was eventually discharged, I guess, but I'm not really sure, for at the 1981 50th Anniversary Homecoming Celebrations, I met him on the base still looking physically fit and very much at home. A lot of former Trentonians chose to live in the town of Trenton after discharge — and Hub may be one of these.

July 21st, 1944 saw one of the largest crowds ever to watch boxing at Trenton — about 3,000, including service personnel and civilians. The card featured bouts between the usual skilled and better-known boxers from the Air Force and Army and these fights were dutifully reported in CONTACT and given top notice. Almost hidden near the end of the report was this item...

"Another bout that created a great deal of interest, especially among the station personnel, was the clash between Firefly Stiles of Edmonton and Wrong-way Lebskin of Toronto, two novices fighting their first bout. Both trained diligently for the last month in an effort to make this, their inaugural, a success. Firefly won a close decision in this encounter."

If ever an event was under-reported this one was. The so-called main bouts provided entertainment for only a few minutes — in the case of the heavyweight fight only a few seconds — but the Stiles-Lebskin fight had provided the station with running speculation, gossip and fun for weeks up to and including the three-round battle.

Moose Matthews, a prominent baseball player and station fireman, had convinced a gullible young associate in the Firehall that he could be some kind of boxer. The problem was to find him an opponent. A brief search led to another young naive airman — my assistant editor, Cpl Alex 'Wrong-way' Lebskin. Neither young airman knew the other but in no time they were being told that each was making disparaging remarks about the other. The predictable and planned happened, i.e., the two must settle their differences in the boxing ring.

News of the impending battle spread through the station, creating much mirth, for neither combatant could be called a fighter by any stretch of the imagination. Interest was so high that when it was learned that the Firefly was receiving secret training from qualified instructors, Station Warrant Officer Silver told me to release Lebskin for an hour each morning and afternoon so that he, too, could receive training.

While Wrong-way was working out against a punching bag in the Sports Hangar one day, SWO Silver arrived on the scene, escorting the Commanding Officer, G/C Bell-Irving, on one of his rounds of inspection. John guided the CO over to Cpl

Lebskin and introduced them to one another — explaining the importance of the upcoming bout. Alex told me about this meeting himself after he returned to our office from his training session. He was quite excited about it and had obviously been impressed by the encounter. It was as though he had been presented to royalty.

When the night of the big bouts arrived, the Station Band was in attendance, as it usually was for major boxing meets. It entertained by playing between each bout but on this occasion the script called for it to play a waltz while the two novices were actually fighting. All part of the fun.

Time came for the Stiles-Lebskin battle. SWO Silver climbed into the ring and announced the contestants, then each came to the centre of the ring at the referee's beckoning and touched gloves.

There were no punches thrown in the first round that I can recall — but then I've seen internationally televised professional fights in which no punches were thrown in the first round, either. What the two men did was spar and, much to the surprise of the crowd, to spar most impressively. The crowd was suddenly silent, as was the band. The two so-called novices, in probably the best physical condition of their lives, had obviously learned a lot in their weeks of training. The expected farce had become a fight.

The second round, however, was something else. Nobody had told Wrong-way that he was supposed to touch gloves with his opponent only at the start of the **first round**. True to his nickname, he approached the centre of the ring in the second and put his gloves forward in the traditional friendly gesture. With his guard down, he promptly got belted in the mouth. I still remember the surprised look on his face, almost forty years later. From then on the fight became a track meet with the Firefly trying to catch up with Wrong-way. I felt sorry for my man but gained a new respect for him. Grossly outweighed by at least twenty-five pounds and with a reach several inches shorter than his opponent's, he showed a lot of guts in just turning up for the fight. The scant space given the bout in the sports reporter's lengthy story about the whole meet was an insult to both fighters.

Some Valiant Men

Among the many thousands of men on the base during wartime there were always some who had already been in action against the enemy overseas. Some were at the station as instructors — or taking the Officers' Admin. Course — or were in the Reselection Centre awaiting reassignment to other trades. Because so many of them had adventurous tales to tell, a few were sent to me to be interviewed and have their stories published in the station paper. The stories were too many and most of them too long to include here. But to mention just a few, there was S/L A.L. de la Haye, DFC, an instructor with Central Flying School, who had been attached to a squadron charged with carrying out strikes against enemy shipping off the Norwegian coast. He had counted among his victims not only ships but flying boats, as well.

A new Station Administration Officer, W/C F.R. Emond, turned up in 1944 and told of service in the U.K., South Africa and Ceylon. On his way from Ceylon to England aboard the Canadian Pacific ship, "Empress of Canada", the ship had been torpedoed and sunk about 500 miles off the African west coast. Over 400 lives were lost in the shark-infested water. Emond was adrift in a boat, with other survivors, for fifteen hours before being picked up by a British destroyer.

On an Admin. Course at Trenton in early 1943 was the already well-known S/L "Moose" Fumerton. He had seen extensive service in the Middle East where his efforts in the defense of Malta won him the DFC and Bar. He had thirteen enemy planes to his credit when he arrived at Trenton. Also taking the Admin. Course at the same time was F/L Jones, DFC, with five downed Huns to his credit.

Another young officer whose exciting story had already been aired over the radio when he reached the base was F/O Stewart Cowan. Flying a Beaufighter in the Mediterranean, he had been part of an attacking force attempting to sink a loaded Axis troopship during the Sicilian invasion. The troopship was accompanied by a strong protecting force of cruisers and destroyers and it was while engaging these that Cowan's starboard propeller was shot off and his port engine hit. Forced to ditch, he and his observer floated around in a rubber dinghy

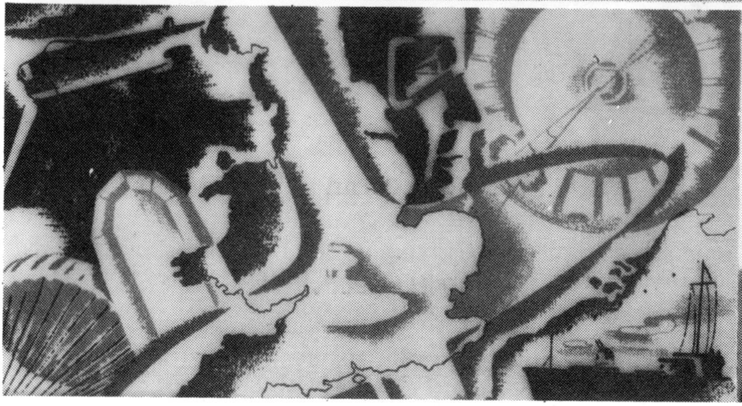

F/O Cowan's Beaufighter is shown being shot down (foreground) in battle in Bay of Naples. Flyers who had to take to rubber dinghys became members of the Goldfish Club. Cowan's card, shown here, depicts nine symbols (see list below).

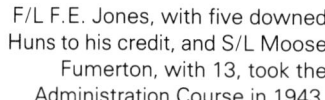

F/L F.E. Jones, with five downed Huns to his credit, and S/L Moose Fumerton, with 13, took the Administration Course in 1943.

Extreme left: LAC Ludwigson, first Norwegian to receive British Military Cross. Left: Cadet Officer Halvorsen, unwilling intruder into tank battle.

On the Goldfish Card: Stirling Bomber, Spitfire, Fighter dinghy, Bomber dinghy, Map of England, Dutch-French Coast, Air Sea Rescue Launch, Air Sea Rescue Plane.

for several hours before being picked up by an Italian seaplane. Transported to Naples as a prisoner-of-war, he later found himself being sent to Germany by rail after Italy signed an armistice. Enroute, Cowan and a British 8th Army officer escaped by throwing themselves from the train as it slowly climbed a steep grade. His leg injured in the fall, Cowan was helped by friendly Italians but had frequent narrow escapes. One of them was a chase by a German officer who fired shots at the fleeing pair from a range of not more than fifty yards. Six weeks from the time of the train escape, the pair reached British lines. Alongside Cowan's photograph in CONTACT, we ran a picture of his Goldfish Club membership card, given to men who had had to take to rubber dinghys when forced down at sea. The card featured nine overlapping symbols and CONTACT's readers were invited to try to recognize them.

To have an aircraft shot out from under you is bad enough but to be forced to bail out and find yourself drifting into the middle of a tank battle is just too much excitement. This was the experience of Cadet Officer Dick Halvorsen who was taking the Ab Initio course at Trenton in 1944, after service in the Middle East. Halvorsen was doing intruder work with the RAF over Libya and on the day he was shot down was acting as protection for his flight.

"It was my unlucky day," he stated. "I spotted four Jerries but when I went to warn my mates I found my R.T. was not working."

He tried to catch up to his flight then, failing that, he broke off to attack the Jerries — downing one before being hit by the others. His plane on fire, Halvorsen bailed out over Knightsbridge where the 8th Army was engaged in a terrific tank battle with Rommel's forces. It was nip and tuck as to which lines he would fall into. Fortunately, a strong wind carried him toward the Allies where Tommies in a Bren gun carrier dashed to his rescue.

Another young flier on the Ab Initio course was Cadet Officer T. Templeman, DFM, who held some sort of record for traveling by "Shank's mare" over 700 miles to safety after being shot down over German-held territory. He was returning from a raid on the Krupp Works at Essen when his plane was hit and the crew had to bail out at a height of only 700 feet over the German-Belgian border. Templeman fractured an ankle in landing but managed to avoid capture and begin his long trek to Gibraltar. Traveling through Belgium and France he eventually reached Spain but in climbing over the mountains fell and fractured his spine. He was captured but later released and flown to England where he spent eight months having the fractured parts of his body recast.

Among men with interesting stories sent to me from the

Reselection Centre, there were always some belonging to the Free French, Belgium, Norwegian and other European air forces. Almost all had fled from their homelands and their tales were of these escapes.

One was LAC Ludwigson, MC, the first Norwegian ever to be honoured with the award of the Military Cross by the British. Ludwigson had been a lieutenant attached as a liaison officer to British troops in Norway. In May, 1940, he was in charge of a small company of British troops when it was discovered they had been cut off from the main body which, during the evacuation, had crossed a river further up. Pursued by the Germans, Ludwigson's party reached the river but only a British pilot and the lieutenant could swim. The river was icy and swollen with snow water. The two swimmers decided to try to get the others across by taking, between them, one man at a time.

The Germans, about 800 yards away, were shooting at them as they plunged into the water, grasping the men they were trying to help across. The fire was maintained each time the swimmers crossed and recrossed. Everyone eventually got across, with the exception of two who were killed and some others who were drowned trying to cross by themselves. The lieutenant then led the party about eleven miles to the coast where they were taken to Scotland on a British ship. After a stint in the Merchant Navy, Ludwigson came to Canada as a potential RCAF pilot.

The "Little Norway" air station at Toronto was the goal for many escaping Norwegians. Some were sent from there to Trenton to take the Flying Instructors Course. Most did not want their names used in stories for fear of reprisal against families still in Norway. One who had fought with the Norwegian ski patrol against the Nazis told of his capture and internment in a prison camp — and of his eventual escape with seven others into neutral Sweden.

Norwegian officials there secured passage for the party on a plane leaving for Russia. Flying high over German-held territory, they arrived in Moscow where friends of the Norwegian government arranged further eastward flights which took them to Alma Ata, a little town on the Russian-Chinese border. They crossed the border into Hami in the heart of the Gobi Desert. Through the good care of a British consul, they then reached the heavily-bombed Chinese capital of Chungking. Then followed a perilous flight over Japanese lines, made during a severe storm in order to avoid enemy aircraft. At Hong Kong, Norwegian government officials arranged passage on a freighter to Los Angeles. From there, the long but safe journey to Toronto was made.

Quite a few Norwegians escaped to Britain in small boats across the North Sea. One at Trenton told of having to make his own perilous way to a certain embarkation point suggested by a well-organized underground. His companions in a twenty-foot boat that was to cross the North Sea were a woman, a tiny girl and eight other men. Dressed as vacationers in order not to arouse suspicious Nazis, the group set out and arrived without mishap at Scotland. Off the Shetland Islands they met other boatloads and heard tales of other groups not so fortunate. Some were swept past the Shetlands into the North Atlantic and were heard of no more.

One story of persistent escape efforts had a sad ending. A young Belgian attending the station's Air Gunners Course in 1943 told how he had fought the Nazis as a WAG in the Belgian Air Force. During the German subjugation of the Low Countries, he fled to France and became a member of the French Air Force. When France was crushed he fled once more. After reaching Bordeaux he was refused permission to leave for England — so discarded his uniform and made his way back to Belgium in civilian garb. In the spring of 1941, he again tried to escape to England. This time, he managed to get to Paris — then traveled southwest to Bordeaux which was the demarcation line separating Occupied France from the Vichy Zone.

There, he was arrested by police but later escaped and made his way toward the Spanish border. Arrested again by Vichy police, he was placed in a concentration camp at Toulouse. He met another young Belgian there and a few days later the two escaped and reached the Mediterranean coast. Joined by two other Belgians, the four succeeded in crossing the Spanish border. The trip across the Pyrenees Mountains took four days and the eighty miles from there to Madrid were covered in forty-eight hours. In Spain, Belgians were taken care of by the British Embassy which arranged for the group to be sent to Gibraltar. While there for five weeks, they met Lord Gort, CO of the fortress. From the historic Rock, there was a comparatively unadventurous journey to England and Canada.

The Belgian was a short young man who, while telling his story, gave me his name and home address in Brussels — in case I were ever there. We could meet, he suggested. Before we went to press with his story and just a few days after he left Trenton, he walked into a propeller at his new base and was killed.

The day the brains came: A/V/M Adelard Raymond, Air Officer Commanding No. 1 Air Command, arrives with part of his staff in January 1945.

Above left: "Getting out" was the thing to do in 1945. The happy faces shown here in front of the Release Office indicate that objective has been achieved.

Above right: F/Sgt Eric Nicol, author and playwright, shown on the Trenton waterfront in 1945.

Left: "So long, gang!" says Cpl Hogan. Personnel waving goodbye was a common sight as demobilization increased in 1945.

Flight Sergeant Eric Nicol

When No. 1 Air Command arrived at Trenton in January 1945 it brought with it a Public Relations Section consisting of F/O Jack Coldwell, son of the CCF (later NDP) leader, F/Sgt Eric Nicol, a blonde whom Nicol has been unable to forget after almost forty years, and some other bodies I can no longer recall.

Nicol, a writer, had developed quite a following through some serious and, more notably, humourous articles in WINGS. One that I've always remembered was "The Cross of Homer Quincey" — a story about a supposedly dimwitted young man from Moose Groin, Saskatchewan who, having looked at the army draft notice he had received in the morning mail, joined the RCAF in the afternoon.

"At the Toronto Manning Depot," Nicol wrote, "a whole new world opened up to Quincey, who had never before taken his pants off in public. His mind was still filled with the burning message of the recruiting poster — 'FLY AND FIGHT WITH THE RCAF!' — but he quickly discovered that Manning Depot was less interested in the fight than in the fly, and life became one long inspection."

Nicol visited Trenton in mid-1944 to write a two-page feature story about the base called "Trenton — Big and Versatile" which appeared in the October WINGS of that year. It was during his visit that we first met. When F/Sgt Nicol turned up with Command in 1945 it seemed like a sensible arrangement for two persons engaged in the same kind of work to team up as roommates. Our room was in the tall barrack block facing the parade square and nearest to the Admin. Building. Nicol had barely unpacked when I put pressure on him to write some of his funny stuff for CONTACT.

He complied by submitting an article about the arrival of No. 1 Command which we published in the first 1945 issue. It was headed, "The Day The Brains Came", a title which seemed to imply that we who were already at Trenton were brainless. This article might have got Nicol off to a bad start at Trenton had he not also submitted a short item which endeared him immediately to everybody in the RCAF who had ever tried to pry materials loose from Equipment Sections. Titled "Stores — The Constipated Cornucopia", it told of the Flight's discovery of the important part which E42s played in total war. He found it impossible to get anything from Stores without one of those Internal Demand and Issue Vouchers. More than that, he learned that if his office was out of the forms, as it was, he still needed an E42 to obtain a new supply of E42s. When told of this by Stores, the Flight went slightly mad. Laughing hysterically, he rushed from the building — but not before noticing that the attending equipment clerk had calmly marked on her E159 sheet, as issued: "Nuts ea. 1".

Nicol displayed such a tremendous sense of humour in getting inside the bureaucracy of the air force that it was no time before almost everybody at Trenton who had ever suffered the frustrations of service life were enthusiastic and ardent readers. Here was a guy able to look at problems we all faced, see something funny in them and write about them. "The Day The Brains Came" was followed by "Parting Is Such Sweet Sorrow", a description of obstructions met by all in getting cleared from a base, and "The Trail Of The 48". The latter was about the boarding of — and riding on — the train assembled by the CNR each weekend to transport hordes of Trentonians to and from Toronto. The trains, described by Nicol as "converted oxcarts which local wags call railway coaches," will be remembered by all wartime Trentonians who crushed their way onto and off those ancient wagons.

Erma Bombeck, the noted columnist whose humourous writings are a weekly feature of the present-day CONTACT, has disclosed that she is not in demand as a public speaker because she can't ad lib. She has to work at writing humour. While Eric Nicol ad libs well today, I can't recall that he was good at it at Trenton. I do know that he would return to his office on many evenings to work hard on his stories. It surprised me, too, to find him just as hardworking and dedicated in writing his personal letters — cutting, adding and rephrasing, honing skills which later, in civilian life, took him to the top as a Canadian humourist and playwright.

Writing, it seemed to me, was a sort of recreational work where Nicol was concerned — yet it did not prevent him from taking advantage of badminton and tennis facilities on the base. He was very good at both sports. I learned firsthand how well he played tennis when I'd be dragged from my comfortable bunk to become his unwilling opponent on the courts. I was glad when he discovered women who played tennis.

Mention of women is a reminder that WDs were among the Flight's most loyal and enthusiastic readers. A story was told about one particular WD who would sit on top of a double-bunk bed and read aloud a Nicol story to a barracks roomful of delighted airwomen. Now and then, I would be accosted on the Main Drag by a gaggle — or giggle — of airwomen bent on finding out from me what the funny Flight was like.

When I passed news of this interest and admiration on to Nicol he was unimpressed. "Insects," he informed me, "are more interesting than women." I didn't agree, of course, but when the next horde of airwomen descended on me, I gave it to them straight. Changing my roommate's remark only slightly, I declared ... "Nicol says that insects are more interesting than **air**women."

Reaction was instant and quite unexpected. Falling back — stunned for a moment, I thought — the women then exploded with laughter, slapping one another on the back and behaving as though I'd just delivered one of the Flight's funniest lines.

Today, obviously embarrassed when reminded of his ungallant insect remark, Nicol vehemently denies ever making it. In an effort to redeem himself he recently advised me that what he actually had said about WDs was that they were "in sex, more interesting women." But that's not the way I heard it and Nicol, on occasion, has credited me with having total recall.

In "Bleeding Can Be Fun", the Flight told of another fairly common wartime experience, the donating of blood — a procedure which he described as "being on draft for democarcy." This was followed by "Markers Can Be People", a story about compulsory drill. "Drill," he wrote, "is like taking castor oil — it may be good for a person, but nobody wants to take it because it means too many darn movements."

Nicol hated drill — especially parades, with good reason. One of his jobs was to write speeches for the Air Vice Marshal at Trenton. He thought it a special indignity when forced to march out onto the parade square and listen to this officer give him his own speech, in the pouring rain.

Beer and liquor were rationed during the war and efforts of rednosed service drinking types to cope with this problem became the subject of "Eighteen Ways To Win Friends", published in September 1945. Targets for drinkers were non-drinkers, of whom Nicol was then one. The goal of the drinkers was to so flatter the non-drinkers that, in appreciation, the temperance-types would hand over their monthly beer and liquor permits to their thirsty admirers. As Nicol wrote — "Without even joining the Ad & Sale Club I had suddenly become a powerful personality; without even improving my bust I was attracting men."

Nicol's parting shot at Trenton was about parting, period. Called "Discharge Of The Light Brigade", he told of thousands of airmen and airwomen whose discharges had come through in late '45. He described how these delighted people went about waving their railway tickets in the faces of those of us left behind, of their hissing at senior NCOs, and of his own frustration in trying to convince the RCAF that it could get along without him. His efforts, however, were fruitful. By the time the article was published in October 1945 he had already left the base.

When a writer is as well-known across Canada as Eric Nicol is today it seems hardly necessary to explain what happened to him after he left Trenton. However, following his discharge he did some teaching of English at the University of British Columbia, wrote columns for the local newspapers and plays for the CBC. 1949 found him in France where he stayed for three years while studying for a degree in literature at the Sorbonne. During this period he was also writing the very popular Bernie Braden show for the BBC. Back in Canada, he has spent his years doing what he likes to do and does best — write. He has a regular column in the Vancouver Province, writes radio and TV scripts, and stage plays. He has written twenty-five books, three of which won the prestigious Stephen Leacock Award for Humour.

During the 1970s and early '80s, Joan Wright, then editor of CONTACT, republished some of Nicol's articles under the heading of "Looking Back" — so during the past few years Eric became as well-known around the Bay of Quinte area for his wartime writing as for his present-day work. Because of this, Major Lorne Johnson, base information officer, decided that a trans-Canada interview of Nicol by telephone would be a worthwhile feature during the 1981 50th Anniversary Homecoming Celebrations. The talk was to be taped — and was — then aired over Quinte area radio stations. On this occasion, in my opinion, the former Flight was a dead loss.

When Nicol was asked, "Have you any recollections of Trenton in the Forties?" the Major was, I'm sure, expecting to hear something of special significance in return. Something like, for instance, the colourful telling about a certain event which would highlight the important part played by the base in winning the war.

What the good Major got, at first, was Nicol remembering "the turtles that inhabited the reedy grass along the Bay" — then the aforementioned "blonde who worked in the Public Relations Office."

As pointed out in my Preface — the passage of time can dim the memory. Nicol's, for sure.

Preparing For After the Brawl

Rehabilitation: To make one capable of becoming a useful member of society again.

This one dictionary definition of the word "rehabilitation" is as good as any when on the subject of preparing service persons to cope once more with civilian life. Even though World War II was a long way from being over there were signs it was going to be won — so rehabilitation became a topic of lively conversation as early as mid-1943 at Trenton Air Station. It was time to start thinking about what would happen after the war.

The Canadian government was beginning to issue news of post-war education and rehabilitation benefits planned for armed forces men and women — and in its June 1943 edition the station paper published its first editorial on the subject in an effort to stimulate thinking about civilian careers.

Corporal Ron Rewbury, a part-timer on CONTACT, wanted to do more than this. Why not, he suggested, help the government by finding out exactly what RCAF men and women planned to do after the war. An exuberant, energetic airman and a former reporter for the Niagara Falls Review, Ron claimed experience in conducting polls. He wanted to poll Trenton's personnel so I told him to go ahead.

Rewbury's system was to make up sets of questionnaires — one for each prominent air force trade — and hand them out to men and women on the base. He became a very busy scribe for he not only had to distribute, then collect the completed questionnaires — he had to compile and analyse them, then write stories on his findings. It kept him out of the wet canteen for a while.

Ron worked so hard and turned in so many stories that the July CONTACT became pretty much a Rehabilitation Issue. "Post-war Security Up To Government" was the front page heading. "Pilots Desire To Stay In Air Force" ... "MT Lads Want To Go Into Business" ... "Air Gunners Want To Be Pilots After The War" ... "Union Scale Theme of Bandsmen" were just a few other headlines. Other articles pointed out that fifty percent of airwomen hoped to continue in the Service ... ditto, the groundcrew trades. Hospital assistants wanted out of the Service, period — most clerks wanted similar civilian positions and so on. We featured many editorials on subjects such as "After The War" and the "Veterans' Land Act".

It was great stuff. So much so that civilian newspapers across Canada reprinted parts of the issue and commented on the findings. A Member of Parliament got up in the House of Commons and, waving a copy of CONTACT, demanded to know what the government intended to do about these post-war desires of the armed forces — effectively, I suppose, assuring Rewbury's findings of a place in Hansard.

Somehow, news of Trenton's poll reached Senator Claude Pepper of the U.S.A., who wrote to CONTACT informing us that his country was working on many measures to assure post-war security. He enclosed a copy of a bill providing for loans to war service persons wishing to complete educations interrupted by the war.

RCAF Station, Trenton was getting publicity galore. Rewbury, as originator of the stories and I, as editor, were basking in the glory of it all. Then a cloud appeared. One day, while walking along the main east-west road on the base, which we called the Main Drag, I was buttonholed by a corporal from the band. How did CONTACT figure out that fifty percent of the bandsmen wanted to make the playing of music their livelihood after the war, he asked. "Fifty percent of us can't play well enough."

Telling him I'd take the matter up with Rewbury I did that, just as soon as I got back to my office. Ron bristled.

"I'm pretty sore at the bandsmen," he explained. "I gave each of them questionnaires but only two turned them in — and one guy said he wanted to make his living in music ... and the other didn't."

"My gawd! What have we done?" I thought. What about all the newspaper publicity — the thundering MP — and the prominent U.S. senator. If the rest of our stories were based on research as flimsy as that behind the bandsmen article, I could be drawn and quartered — court-martialed — maybe sent to Goose Bay.

Rewbury stayed calm. He assured me that all the other stories were O.K. Apprehensively, I took his word for it. But for months afterwards I sometimes felt a little sick, thinking about what might have happened had the true story on the bandsmen poll got out.

Once rehabilitation became a major concern of the government everybody at Trenton started to get into the act. Our padres, and we had six, took a broad view, urging not only

102 / Preparing For After the Brawl

planning for individual civilian careers but for global peace and a better Canada, too. They wanted us to do more than plan ... they wanted us to pray. CONTACT featured a monthly column headed, "The Sky Pilot Says", and in one issue it carried the subheading, "Think, Work, Pray, Now - About After The War". Some of us, conscious of the depression years leading up to the war and with no great job prospects for after it, probably did just that.

By 1944, information about post-war planning was flooding in from the government — reaching station paper editors and educational officers right across Canada. Trenton's educational officer in April 1943 was F/O S. Tooke and he headed a rehabilitation feature in that month's station paper with this little World War I ditty...

> "When this awful war is over,
> Oh, how happy I shall be,
> When I get my civvy clothes on,
> No more soldiering for me."

Anything to get personnel looking ahead.

F/O Tooke then went on to outline some benefits planned by the government — one of which called for a sixty-five dollar clothing allowance for each veteran upon discharge. CONTACT decided to conduct another of its famous polls on this subject. The result? The clothing allowance was considered too stingy. One-hundred dollars would be more like it, stated sixty-four percent of the base airmen and airwomen — while thirty-three percent (Beau Brummells, all) wanted two-hundred dollars. The government eventually decided to pay one-hundred dollars. Chalk one up for polls and protests.

As months went by, more and more columns about rehabilitation appeared in the station paper — some providing government-issued information, others in the form of quizzes to stimulate thinking.

In 1943, with accommodation assured, three square meals a day, everything found and the end of the war still a long way away, there was a tendency to put off thinking about the future. But attitudes were changing. In 1945, CONTACT published a little poem which pretty much told the story:

> Airmen who wish to be a hero
> Number practically zero.
> Those who wish to be civilians
> Number way up in the millions.

That this wasn't always so was shown by CONTACT's first poll on rehabilitation in 1943 when forty-seven percent answered

Preparing For After the Brawl / 103

"No" to the question: "Do you plan to remain in the Air Force at the conclusion of the war?"

By May, 1944, just ten months later, the number of those who wanted out had risen to eighty-four percent.

Government information and CONTACT's warnings to make peacetime plans were having their effect. The new attitudes were more or less summed up in this little comment in the station paper:

"It isn't so much the rationing,
Or taxes, or talk of inflation;
The problem really worrying us
Is this thing called duration."

Canada's Wartime Information Board was the source for most of the government-distributed literature. I decided the place was worth a visit. Perhaps there might be additional material available that Trenton wasn't getting — items that might interest our men and women.

At the Wartime Information Board in Ottawa I was introduced to Captain Gordon Lunan, a friendly army officer who was to gen me up on all the available booklets, magazines and other material.

Captain Lunan was a Britisher so a spot of tea was in order before we settled down to business. One or two other visits to Ottawa and the friendly captain followed.

When I took my discharge in late 1945, I became editor of TORCH magazine, a veterans' publication. Captain Lunan informed me by letter from Ottawa that WIB literature would still be available to me in my new work. He also sent little scribbled notes about some of the authors of WIB articles, pointing out that a number of them were scientists. The name of one of the scientists was Professor Boyer.

Shortly afterwards, in early 1946, Igor Gouzenko, a cipher clerk in the Russian Embassy in Ottawa, defected and exposed the operation of a Communist spy ring within Canada. As I read the startling front-page story in Toronto's Globe and Mail I looked down the list of exposed spies. Heading it was Fred Rose, a Communist Member of Parliament. Farther down, I was shocked to see the name of the helpful Captain Lunan, who was reported to be the ring's go-between. The name of Professor Boyer was also on the list.

Lunan and Boyer were both sentenced to five years of imprisonment. MP Fred Rose served six years and then returned to his native Poland.

At its peak, December 1943, the strength of the RCAF was 232,632 (including over 17,000 WDs). By June, 1945, Ottawa was issuing figures on demobilization and in the July

CONTACT, under the heading, "Assignment Home" we reported that the RCAF was to be pared from the then strength of 165,000 to 100,000.

Meanwhile, on April 16, 1945, a perplexed Winston Churchill, in memorandums to his Secretary of State for Air and Chief of Air Staff, wondered why the BCATP in Canada had been broken up so abruptly. The nucleus, he wrote, should have been preserved.

At Trenton, wild rumours about demobilization abounded so, to spike them, the station paper obtained and published true facts pertaining to the problem of applying for and securing immediate release.

Discharge! Suddenly everybody — or nearly everybody — wanted out of the air force and those still left on the base looked with envy at the large numbers of men and women leaving every month.

Eventually, all who wanted out, and some who didn't, found themselves on Civvy Street. There, thanks to Canada's generous rehabilitation grants and, we hope, the preparatory help they had received from CONTACT's columns, most were able to make the adjustment from the country-club-like life they had enjoyed at Trenton to the rigours of civilian life.

THERE'LL ALWAYS BE A K.T.S.

MOPPED UP!   HOPPED UP!   GRIN UP!   CHIN UP!

Top to bottom:

Cartoonist F/L Rickard shows progression of emotions by washed-out aircrew member as he enters and departs from the Aircrew Reselection Centre.

The famous Milton Caniff was a valued contributor of armed forces cartoons. His creation, "Lace", was a popular morale builder.

Slipstream Sam was the author's creation, a direct result of an officer's order to "Do some cartoons".

Trenton airmen were such enthusiastic fans of the WOLF cartoons that their U.S. Army creator, Cpl Sansone, drew this one specifically for Trenton men and women.

Do Some Cartoons

During the 1930s, while I was working as a salesman in Eaton's Toronto store chinaware department, a huge shipment of dishes, steins and mugs arrived from England. Each piece was decorated with a cartoon by Bruce Bairnsfather. Following an advertisement announcing the shipment's arrival, people flocked to the store and just about cleared the shelves and tables of Bairnsfather china in a few days.

Bruce Bairnsfather, artist and journalist, was serving with his regiment, the Warwickshires, in World War I when, in 1916, he was shifted to the British War Office. He started to do humourous drawings of army life which, at first, made him a subject of official censure. The drawings, however, proved extremely popular, especially those showing life in the trenches, and particularly those containing the character, "Old Bill", used to typify the spirit of the British infantryman. This lesson on the importance of cartoons in warfare, and the impression they left with people for years afterwards, was recalled by me shortly after I joined the staff of Trenton's station magazine.

Considered as strictly a peacetime occupation, cartooning packed a wallop in WWII that was aimed by and against the enemy. The RAF and RCAF quickly learned the value of cartoons and lost no time in obtaining men to do the work. Comic characters such as Hooper's Pilot Officer Prune of the RAF did much to point out, in the flying training manual "Tee Emm", the wisdom of adhering to training instructions.

Hooper's counterpart in the RCAF was Hugh Rickard. Cartoons done by Rickard in his spare time came first to the attention of S/L Baxter at Brandon, where they appeared in the station magazine. Rickard was in training as aircrew but like a lot of us who didn't make it, he ended up at Trenton's Aircrew Reselection Centre. Still turning out cartoons in his spare time — and he had plenty of it while awaiting reselection — he found them put to use by S/L Massey and other KTS officers. Massey didn't stop there. "Ricky's" good work was brought to the attention of Headquarters in Ottawa, with the result that Rickard got a commission and "Ricky" cartoons played a valuable part during the rest of the war, educating and building morale throughout the Service.

SERVICE TYPES by F/Sgt Ed Hand

THE STARTLED FAWN OR NEW P/O – casting furtive eyes for salutes. Everything is shiny new but he tries to appear casual. Can hardly wait to get home to take the wire out of his hat. Hopes he runs into his old discip from Manning Pool.

HAPPY IN THE SERVICE – Thinks drill and P.T. is fun and his corporal a swell fellow. Is very busy attending all the "Y" doin's and can't see why fellows get cheesed off. Oh yes, he's been in about six months.

HE'S HAD IT, YOU KNOW – That tired mushroom he's wearing used to be a fairly sharp chapeau. He left home as a rosy cheeked boy, but someone told him you have to scare the Nazis to death so he grew the shrubbery under his beak. His decorations show a good job but he should have taken his uniform off ONE night since '40.

VERY OPSY – "Knows the score." Knows K.R. backwards and can quote it. Knows Sec. 4-44 but has a crime sheet in three editions. Is browned off and expects you to feel the same way. Can be located any time after six on defaulters' parade, and proud of it.

ADMIN TYPE – Hat square on according to C.A.P. something or other. Has worked his way up from P/O to F/O the hard way (over prone airmen). Will stop at nothing to see that justice is done – providing it gets to his O.C.

SO, YOU AIN'T GOT A PASS, EH? – or What happened to the peacetime bogeyman. He joined the SP's. Usually seven feet tall, he can be found any time throttling some scrawny A.C. with a non-issue collar button on. Actually, he's quite harmless if you treat him right – and often.

DIRECT ENTRY F/Sgt Works and Bricks. Salutes every-one from LAC up with one of those arthritic-type hands. Wears his uniform as if it were made for him – and two other guys. Not much to look at but oh, so necessary.

THE P.T. AND D. The expression stayed on his face when he found out he'd washed out on his G.D. course. Believes all ranks tremble when he approaches. Has the shiniest buttons, boots and seat in his pants on the Station. Took his ten-weeks' course in Munich.

F/Sgt Ed Hand was a PTI at Trenton. These impressions of various RCAF types were made in 1945.

Early in 1942, I was producing drawings for the headings of various stories and news sections in CONTACT. One day the editor, an officer, said to me:

"Do some cartoons."

"I'm not a cartoonist," I advised him.

"You are now," he replied.

At first, I found that the toughest part of cartooning was coming up with ideas. The job required much concentration which was difficult to achieve amid the usual bustle in the magazine office. I decided to retire to my barracks room bunk and lie on it, awaiting inspiration. In spite of remarks about goofing off from other members of the staff, I found that once one idea came, others with some connection to the preceding one would follow and pretty soon I'd have several ideas for cartoons. Later, I began to see potential cartoon material in just about every base activity and the work soon became easier and pleasurable. Partway through 1942 I developed a cartoon character called "Slipstream Sam" and later turned out a comic strip based on the same character. Happy in the work, I became even happier when one day I was shown an article from The Toronto Star in which the noted sports editor, Andy Lytle, who apparently received copies of CONTACT, described me as "another Bairnsfather around the Trenton corner."

A good fifteen to twenty years after the war I was having a drink after a golf game with John Collyer, who had been a headquarters sergeant at Trenton during the war. He was later commissioned and sent overseas where he served as an administrative officer with No. 419 (Moose) Squadron. I'm a habitual doodler and was scribbling away on a paper napkin when John smiled across at me and said, "Draw Slipstream Sam" — another lesson demonstrating the lasting impression that cartoons can have.

There was a physical training instructor at Trenton in '42 who did cartooning and who was active, also, in the station's theatrical shows. Many ex-air force men and women may remember him for his later work as a star comedian with the RCAF entertainment show, "Blackouts", which played at bases across Canada and overseas. His name was Fran Dowie and he signed his cartoons with just his first name, Fran. Dowie was contributing to a full page of cartoons in CONTACT called "Cartoon Corner" but in the October issue, following the arrival of airwomen on the base, he, too, developed a comic strip. His was based on amusing activities of airwomen and he called it "Sergeant Sally".

One never knows when or where one may run into former Trentonians, which isn't surprising considering the many thousands of men and women who have gone through the base. In 1958, I was sitting in a theatre in Brighton, England waiting for the performance to begin when I noticed on the program an act called "Fran Dowie — Canadian Funster". There couldn't be two Canadian Fran Dowies, I thought, and sure enough, when the act came due, a stouter version of Trenton's former PTI appeared on stage. A note sent via an usher brought an invitation to go backstage. There, I learned that Dowie traveled the British Isles and Scandinavian countries, singing western songs in what he hoped he still had — a Canadian accent. I believe he is a theatrical agent in western Canada today.

There must have been an abundance of cartoonists — frustrated and otherwise — in the RCAF because, in no time, without even soliciting any, CONTACT became inundated with cartoons. Readers seemed to like the cartoons so pretty soon we had to devote two whole pages to them, while at the same time publishing a notice begging contributors not to submit any more.

In 1942, the Americans were well into the war and to help their base and service newspapers authorities set up what was called the Camp Newspaper Service. Something like a regular newspaper syndicate, it provided up-to-the-minute news and pictorial features, aircraft recognition charts and, of course, cartoons. I wrote to CNS, pointing out that since both our countries were fighting the same enemies, it would be nice if they would make their CNS services available to Trenton's CONTACT. Being Yanks, their response was, "Sure thing."

From CNS, we got two great cartoon features. The first, drawn by U.S. Sgt Leonard Sansone, was about a soldier with a head of a wolf and a one-track mind that led, always, to women. LIFE magazine devoted two-and-a-half pages to a feature about "The Wolf". The cartoon became so popular with CONTACT readers that when we once left it out of the paper we received complaints for weeks afterwards. Trenton personnel, not familiar with our arrangement with CNS, wondered why the Wolf always appeared in a U.S. army uniform — so we shot off a request to Sansone who obliged with a cartoon drawn especially for airmen and airwomen at Trenton ... showing their favourite character in a very authentic version of an RCAF "Acey Deucy" uniform. Which brings us to the second great U.S. feature we used, a comic strip by the famous Milton Caniff.

Caniff was the originator of the well-known civilian strip, "Terry and the Pirates" — followed later by the strip, "Steve Canyon". Categorized as 4F and unfit for military service, Caniff went to the U.S. War Department and offered to supply a wartime comic strip based on a very attractive and seductive gal named "Lace" whose contribution to the war effort consisted of trying to raise the morale of troops, individually and en masse. The spicy strip was called "Male Call" and it was

The station paper was swamped with cartoons. Here's a typical page including contributions from eight different cartoonists.

as popular at Trenton as it was in the U.S. Caniff was a stickler for authenticity and when he started to work Canadian characters into the strip he requested and received from Canadian headquarters service uniforms from which he could copy details he felt necessary in his drawings.

Apart from "Ricky", Fran Dowie, the two U.S. specialists and me, there were many cartoonists at Trenton who entertained on the pages of CONTACT. Some scrawled their signatures so carelessly that it was difficult to read them — but among some of the readable ones I remember were Mike, Oz, Carr, Alaska and Ray Wade. Because of the transient nature of the RCAF population, especially among trainees, some airmen were on the base only long enough to draw and submit cartoons, and were often posted elsewhere before their work could appear in print. One fine cartoonist who popped up regularly in late 1944 and '45, though, was F/Sgt Eddie Hand who was, I think, on the Trenton staff as a PTI.

In mid-1945, with the war in Europe over, war efforts and propaganda were aimed at bringing about the defeat of Japan. The Canadian government, as part of a plan to promote the Ninth Victory Loan campaign, came up with a poster contest. Rene Kulbach, a fine base artist and muralist, F/Sgt Hand and yours truly were told to submit entries from Trenton. Full of patriotic fervour and with our eyes set, of course, on the $100 prize, the three of worked long hours into the nights on our posters, each of which dealt with the necessity of buying bonds in order to knock out the Japanese. Less than a week later, the Japanese surrendered and our posters became superfluous. It is not stretching things to report that the effect of the atom bomb was felt in more ways than one as far away as RCAF Station, Trenton.

There is evidence of all kinds that cartoons were popular in wartime, perhaps even more popular than in peacetime. At Trenton, we were told this many times. In fact, some persons even wrote to the station paper explaining that they not only enjoyed the cartoons themselves, they sent them home to their families who also enjoyed them.

In addition to the entertaining and morale-building contribution made by cartoons, the fact that comically illustrated instructions register on the minds of readers more easily than sets of complicated rules was proven in wartime, just as it had previously been proven in peacetime. The farseeing artists and officials who started the trend back in World War I led the way for others into a field which made a valuable contribution towards the successful completion of World War II.

In 1943, Jack Boothe, well-known editorial cartoonist of Toronto's Globe and Mail, visited the base and left behind these impressions of some well-known officers.

Some officers responsible for success of 3rd Victory Loan Drive. From l. to r.: F/O Wooley, F/O Sheppard, F/O Sheddon, F/L Harris, F/L Barton and F/L Lamport, famous later on as "Lampy", Toronto's mayor. Below: Airmen and airwomen lined up to publicize 4th Victory Loan Drive.

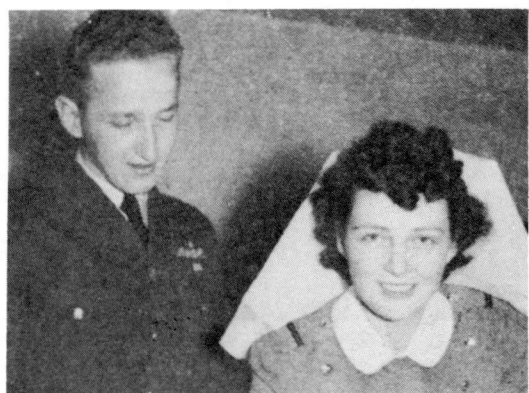

Above left shows LAC and Mrs. Howard Ross, stars in the first all-air force wedding. Alongside, F/L G. Maynard and Nursing Sister Esther Miller, first to take wedding vows in the Officers' Mess.

Remember these athletes: From l. to r. are: Roy Conacher, Boston Bruins; Wally Stanowski, Toronto Maple Leafs; Ron Gunner of the U.K.'s famous QPR soccer team; Eddie Bush, Detroit Red Wings; Johnny Quilty, Montreal Canadiens.

Victory Bonds for Victory

"Why should we help finance the war as well as fight it" was the reaction of some of the armed forces when they were asked in 1942 to participate in the purchase of Victory Bonds. Even some politicians spoke out against the idea — suggesting that men and women in the armed forces were doing enough by joining the services. Fortunately, this was not the prevailing mood, especially among men and women at Trenton. Officers and airmen on the base had sense enough to realize that if victory was to be won, money for the purchase of necessary equipment must be found.

It took huge amounts of money to finance the war — money for tanks, guns, planes, ships and thousands of other costly items. Canada was spending $3.3 billion on the war in 1942 — a colossal sum for a nation of only 11,000,000 people. Financing through taxes was not providing enough so the government introduced Victory Bonds — selling them in twice-yearly campaigns. The government rightly claimed that citizens and the armed forces were not being asked to give money but to LEND it, at a three percent interest rate, too. How did the sales campaigns at Trenton make out?

Trenton was asked to raise $10,000 in the second campaign held in early 1942, the first campaign in which the armed forces participated. This turned out to be a ridiculously modest quota, for Trenton responded by purchasing $42,000 worth of bonds.

Encouraged by this, campaign officials raised Trenton's quota to $30,000 for the Third Campaign held in late 1942. G/C F.S. McGill, Commanding Officer, set up a committee of officers to plan the raising of this amount. One of the members was F/L A.A. Lamport who, in later years, gained fame as "Lampy", mayor of the City of Toronto and the driving force behind introduction of Sunday sports in that city. To stimulate interest among base personnel, a huge boxing show was put on, a station "Open House Day" held, and planes flew in formation over the station, dropping leaflets.

For every $10,000 which an armed forces base raised, a special Victory Loan Flag was awarded. When the Third Campaign closed, Trenton had fifteen of the flags flying from its flagpole — representing purchases of $153,500 worth of bonds. Five-hundred percent over the top.

Objectives set for Trenton continued to grow — and the station continued to surpass them. To do this, all sorts of shows, activities and contests were held.

The campaign for the Fourth Victory Loan was an interesting one. Kicked off with a message in CONTACT from G/C McBurney, CO, the theme was — "We did it before and we can do it again." Did we? Our quota had been bumped up to $125,000. Trenton subscribed $235,950 — a whopping sum that represented nine percent of the total bonds purchased by all of No. 1 Training Command.

CONTACT carried two interesting photographs in connection with this campaign. In one, hundreds of airmen and airwomen were lined up on the parade square to form the Roman numeral IV. Women made the figure "1" by lining up in four groups — three short ones and a long one — to spell out the Morse letter "I", used then as a Victory sign. Men from Headquarters and the Air Gunners School formed the "V" of the Roman numeral IV. Viewed from the air or the top of the Administration Building, from where a photograph was taken, the formation was perfect. SWO Silver claimed to have lost ten pounds lining it up.

Another photograph was used to give some idea of the international set-up at Trenton that ganged up on the Axis in the form of Victory Bond purchases. Three airmen from the Aircrew Reselection Centre and two airwomen were shown, each holding a purchased bond and each representing a different country. Their countries were Belgium, Chile, Great Britain, Netherlands and the U.S.A.

One of the contests I shall never forget was a challenge from the officers that they would purchase three bonds to every one bought by senior NCOs. The settings were two smokers, one held in the Officers' Mess, the other in the Sergeants' Mess. Telephone communication took place to keep track of the score. Handling the telephone at the Sergeants' Mess was SWO John Silver. Every time word came that the officers were nudging ahead, John would roar above the din of songs, shouts and clinking glasses ... "The officers have bought another bloody bond. Who'll buy one here?"

Caught up in the competitiveness of the situation and too well fortified by beer, I raised my hand too many times and yelled ... "I'll buy another one, John!"

Completion of the night's big do found the senior NCOs winners by a slight margin and Trenton's Victory Loan effort richer by several thousands of dollars. Morning brought the news that I'd signed up to buy $700 worth of bonds. It not only wiped out the modest bank account I had in Toronto, I had to sign up under the Payroll Savings Plan to meet the rest of my

116 / Victory Bonds for Victory

obligation. I was broke for seven months.

By the time the Fourth and future Victory Bond Campaigns rolled around, a great deal of publicity regarding the importance of preparing adequate postwar rehabilitation plans was being distributed. Airmen and airwomen could see that a financial backlog in the form of Victory Bonds could play a big part in their postwar plans and this had quite an effect on the campaigns.

The theme for the fifth Campaign was "Speed the Victory" and Trentonians responded by knocking their $160,000 quota for a loop — purchasing $229,500 worth of bonds.

A musical hit parade and other events helped make the sixth a success. In addition, a contest was held, for the first time, pitting South Side station units against the North Side. Each pledged to raise $100,000 to meet the station's quota of $200,000. Their contributions raised $304,450.

Everybody who was on the base in the fall of 1944 will remember the Seventh Victory Loan Campaign for the famous visitors who helped out by entertaining at great concerts and other events. Their efforts, together with an unprecedented display of enthusiasm by all station personnel, resulted in purchases of bonds totaling $477,300 — an amount which was never surpassed and which won for Trenton the Command Victory Loan Flag.

Heading the entertainers were Hollywood stars Carol Bruce and Hume Cronyn. Among other popular entertainers were Bert Pearl and organist Kathleen Stokes of radio's famous "Happy Gang". Impersonator Joe Murphy, talented dancer Zena Cheevers, Lois Spence and Frosia Gregory were others who helped. One other very notable contributor was F/L Jackie Rae, who had returned from overseas with a DFC and who, in the early 1980s, is making musical history with his famous "Spitfire Band", recreating the big band sound of the 1940s.

As if music and dancing were not enough, the hardworking Victory Loan Committee also staged the first professional wrestling bouts ever held on the base, featuring, among others, Whipper Billy Watson, the British Empire Champion. Watson is today still active in a role as a champion for Canada's physcially disabled children.

The war was drawing to a close when the Eighth Victory Loan Campaign was launched in April 1945. Nos. 1 and 3 Training Commands had moved to Trenton to form No. 1 Air Command. Although the base strength was dropping, officers, airmen and airwomen continued to pile up purchases of bonds. The base had two objectives set for it — one of $175,000 to be reached by the RCAF Station, the other of $80,000 the goal of the Administrative Unit of No. 1 Air Command. Entertainment was again a big help in creating interest — with Metropolitan

Opera stars Margaret Speaks and John Dudley highlighting a grand musical evening.

When the campaign concluded, Trenton had beaten its quota with $221,900 while No. 1 ACHQ had set the high in No. 1 Air Command with a magnificent $433,950.

In the seven Victory Bond campaigns conducted on the base, Trenton units were asked to purchase about one million dollars worth of bonds. What the base units actually bought was $2,095,900 worth. Once more, Trenton had shown Canada, just as it still shows today, that it is always more than ready to accomplish that which is asked of it.

Cpl. Alex "Wrongway" Lebskin

On my too-few visits to Vancouver, I always look up an old friend, Ken Scrimger, who was a headquarters NCO at Trenton before being posted overseas in 1944. We are never very far into our reminiscing before Ken will ask, "Remember Wrong-way Lebskin?"

Even if I wanted to forget Alex Lebskin, it would be difficult, for he not only worked closely with me on the station paper, his behaviour could leave an indelible impression on even the most forgetful of minds.

Alex Lebskin was a bandsman by trade — a drummer in the station trumpet band. With an unbelievable penchant for getting into trouble — though not serious trouble — he was under the disciplinary eye of SWO John Silver when I first met him.

When his daily duties with the band were over, Alex had to report to the SWO's office where he would be given chores which would, it was hoped, keep him out of mischief. One of these chores was the polishing of brass doorknobs of all the offices in the Administration Building. There were a lot of doors in the building and, of course, twice as many doorknobs. Sometimes, while sitting at my desk trying to write an article, I would be distracted by the rattling of the office's outside doorknob, as Alex cleaned it. A minute or two later he would open the door a little and half-enter the office in order to clean the inside knob. It would be rattle, rattle, rattle — an annoying intrusion to somebody trying to concentrate. One day, when the CONTACT doorknobs had been rattled and polished five times in just a few hours, I called Alex into my office and asked in unkindly terms if such devotion to duty was necessary.

Alex told me he was interested in what I was doing — so, needing some help at the time, I discussed with Sgt Major Silver the possibility of employing Lebskin on CONTACT. The discussion was over in no time. Recognizing an unexpected opportunity to rid himself of a problem, the SWO agreed wholeheartedly and steered me out of his office — all the time patting me on the back as though I had suddenly become his friend for life.

What Alex lacked in journalistic experience when he joined CONTACT he more than made up for with enthusiasm. At the slightest hint there was was story somewhere, he would grab pad and pencil and almost run to wherever the source of news might be. In less time than anticipated, he was writing interesting stories and headings.

Sometimes, though, he would get a little mixed up as to who and what was news. One example of this occurred during his early days on the magazine when he was sent on an assignment requiring that photographs be taken. He took off with a photographer and later reported that all had gone well. The next day, when prints from the Photographic Section arrived on my desk, Alex, the reporter, was shown to be up front and centre in every photograph. Bellowing at him to stay out of the photographs from then on, I felt that this might be the first of many signs indicating that Lebskin could, unintentionally, turn me into a new type of war casualty.

Four or five months after joining the staff, however, Alex had become such a useful contributor that I felt he should be given a little help. His rank was LAC so I thought things might be easier for him when interviewing officers and NCOs if he, himself, were an NCO.

When I entered the SWO's office with my suggestion, I was met with a roar of disapproval from Sgt Major Silver. However, after he calmed down, John saw merit in the idea and promised to do something about it.

A short time later, on a Friday, John Silver asked me to send Lebskin to him. Sure that he was headed for the usual dressing down, Alex later returned to our office, all smiles and clutching two sets of corporal's stripes in his hand. His first act as Corporal (unpaid) was to pull rank on somebody in Clothing Stores and have his stripes sewn on before leaving for Toronto that day to show them off.

The stripes went over big at home. The only persons who worried more about Alex than me were his parents, of whom he was the only child. Stripes were an indication to them that he was staying out of trouble and Alex apparently gave me some credit for this phenomenon. He asked me to drop in to see his father when I was next on leave in Toronto. Lebskin Sr. owned and ran a drugstore on the east side of Yonge Street, between Dundas and Gerrard Streets. When I complied with Alex's request, the father not only greeted me with open arms, he thrust half-a-dozen bright civilian ties into my hands. What I was supposed to do with civilian ties when in uniform and in the middle of a war, I don't know. I figured they were given in lieu of some kind of medal. Subsequent pop-ins to see the grateful

Mr. Lebskin brought more ties, so that upon discharge I not only did not have to dip into my clothing allowance to buy any, I had almost enough to set up a small shop.

Alex loved airwomen and at Trenton he spent much of his off-duty time with them — telling them so. How much he loved them was brought home to me most surprisingly one night. I had gone to Toronto that day to see if I could get my medical category upgraded and, having failed, was in a bad mood when I returned to the station about midnight. As I went through the guardhouse I decided to go over to the Admin. Building to see if any new stories had been left on my desk. I unlocked the office door and switched on the light. There, startled beyond belief, was Cpl Lebskin and one of the prettiest airwomen on the base. Before I could give vent to my feelings, the embarrassed couple rushed past me to freedom. The next morning, Alex turned up at the office, completely unabashed — and behaving as though the previous night's incident was all my fault.

"Who the hell," he complained, "would expect you to turn up at the office at that hour?"

On New Year's Eve, 1982, I attended a surprise party for the former Cpl Lebskin, who was to celebrate his sixtieth birthday the following day. During the evening, when I mentioned the possibility of writing this book, Alex asked — "Are you going to tell how I got the name 'Wrong-way'?"

I certainly am. The occasion was a farewell smoker given by the Sergeants' Mess to honour G/C R.E. McBurney, who was turning over command of the base to G/C A.D. Bell-Irving, in order to take up duties overseas.

Because of the Scottish ancestry of both Commanding Officers, the Sergeants' Mess Committee decided to inject a little Scottish atmosphere into the proceedings. A flight sergeant, Forbes Wilson, had previously entertained with the playing of bagpipes at a Victory Loan Concert. He had been accompanied by bass drummer, LAC Don Wagner, of German ancestry, and a Jewish side drummer, Alex Lebskin. This odd three-man Highland Band was recalled for duty at the smoker.

The script called for the pipe band members to march into the Mess, led by Lebskin, and to stand at the back of the room, playing their hearts out. Bagpipe music, with banging bass and side drum, is bad enough when performed within the confines of a low-ceilinged Mess hall. Add to that the raucous shouting of boisterous NCOs and the clinking of glasses and we had what seemed like bedlam. Towards the close of the performance, the piper indicated with a nod of his head that Lebskin should lead the band out of the hall. Mistaking the nod as a signal to march up the main aisle to the head table, Alex proceeded to do this — all the while banging away at his drum and enjoying himself no end. The other two-thirds of the band had, by this time, left the hall. When the NCOs realized what was happening they all tried to point out the error to Lebskin by shouting — "Wrong way! Wrong way!" ... while at the same time laughing their heads off. Alex couldn't hear the shouts for the banging of his drum and it was not until he reached the head table that he saw there was no place else to go. With taunts of "Wrong way" shouted at him from all sides, he beat a hasty and embarrassed exit from the hall.

That night, the departing CO was presented with a framed photographic layout of highlights of his tenure at Trenton. Cpl Lebskin received his new name.

If Cpl Wrong-way Lebskin was in favour of a project, he became an enthusiastic and tireless worker. A group of airmen once formed a committee to plan a corn and wiener roast which was to be held at Presqu'ile Point, a provincial park picnic area in Lake Ontario, south of Brighton. Essential to the success of this event, of course, was having enough liquor. Today, this would be no problem. In wartime, it loomed as a very large one — for liquor was rationed. Each person was issued a permit entitling the owner to buy one bottle a month. It was decided that somebody would have to canvas all known non-drinkers and talk them out of their permits for that particular month.

Lebskin claimed that the job required someone with the skill of a con artist and volunteered for it. Great! In no time Wrong-way was arriving daily at the CONTACT office displaying new evidence of his talent in the form of more liquor permits. Permits were not enough, though. They had to be transformed into bottles — and this meant trips to the liquor store in the nearby town of Belleville. No sweat! Cpl Lebskin would hie himself over to the main gate, waving a large empty envelope he claimed had to reach CONTACT's printer in Belleville ... right away! Sensing an emergency, service policemen would obligingly stop the first vehicle going east to make sure the corporal received a lift into town. It surprised me that the service policemen never wondered why the corporal made so many trips into Belleville carrying one large flat envelope and returned so often carrying several round ones. Perhaps one of them was on the committee.

The great day of the picnic arrived. Alex had done his job well. There was ample liquor so he decided to test some of it. By the time that trucks were loaded with airmen and airwomen, ready to depart for the picnic, Cpl Lebskin was also loaded. He was, in fact, out cold. Tossed into one of the trucks like so much baggage he and the cavalcade of picnickers swept out of the main gate, headed for the picnic grounds. I wasn't at this event but somebody told me it was a great party. It wasn't Lebskin, for he was still out of this world when the trucks swept back through the main gate at midnight to deposit their human

122 / Cpl. Alex "Wrongway" Lebskin

cargoes at various barracks doors. The next day, all Wrong-way had to remind himself of the huge contribution he had made toward the success of the project was a colossal hangover.

As the war drew to a close, many of us began to wonder how we would get along in civilian life — whether we would get jobs and what kind. Because of his enthusiasm, aggressiveness and willingness to tackle anything, the only person I was sure would do O.K was Alex. My confidence in his ability to make out in the competitive civilian world has been fully justified. After a stint as a reporter for the Ontario Port Hope Guide — a job at which he displayed his usual enthusiasm so evident at Trenton he set about studying in Toronto to become a druggist. After graduating successfully, however, he found he could make more money selling jewellery. And he found he could make even more money selling jewellery if he sold for more than one firm. This he does, to this date. The icing on his cake, though, is the sales territory he has carved out for himself during our long, cold and hard winters ... the tropical islands of the Caribbean. Obviously, Wrong-way handled "civvy street" the right way. Though suffering from multiple sclerosis today, he continues to insist that both his service and civilian lives have been a piece of cake.

Among outstanding personalities of the entertainment world who performed at Trenton, perhaps the most frequent visitor was Miss Jean Dickenson of Metropolitan Opera and radio fame.

Below is Mart Kenney, another popular visitor, being thanked for a performance by G/C McBurney.

At the bottom right is movie star Carol Bruce, today's Momma Carlson. At the left is G/C Bell-Irving. That's the Canadian, international stage star, Hume Cronyn on the right.

Inset is Ruth Draper, famous actress, who gave a remarkable presentation of characterizations.

Bottom left shows LAW Kay McBride receiving autographs from Bert Pearl and Kathleen Stokes of radio's popular "Happy Gang".

Below left is "The Spirit of 1942" in the ample person of Kate Smith, who invaded the base with her show that year. Darling of the airwaves to millions of listeners, she captured the station single-handedly with her singing and million dollar personality. Who would have thought then, that almost 40 years later her voice would provide the inspiration needed by Philadelphia Flyers in their quest for the Stanley Cup?

Troupers at Trenton

As most of those who served in the armed forces know, a large number of persons in civilian life gave freely of their time to entertain troops across Canada and overseas. Sometimes these people, amateurs mostly, worked at their jobs by day and rehearsed, traveled and performed at night. Others were top Canadian and American professional artists taking time out from their normal theatrical or night club duties to help keep up the morale of service men and women.

Trenton was a fortunate air base for it not only received an abundance of entertainment by outsiders during the war years, it got most of the best.

Many of the civilian entertainment groups were sponsored by firms, with their employees doing the actual entertaining. Most of the shows included a variety of acts ranging from individual singers or singing groups and musicians to dancers, magicians and comedy skits. One of the many groups that came to Trenton was the "Lowney Caravan" (the chocolate people), which put on a show produced by the still-very-well-known Harry "Red" Foster of Toronto. It was the first outdoor show on wheels visiting the armed forces. Other groups were the Red, White and Blue Revue (Bell Telephone employees), the Lifebuoy Follies (Lever Bros.) and the Inglis Revue (John Inglis Co.). Two Eaton revues, put on by employee groups called "The Masquers", came from the Montreal and Toronto stores and showed a very high degree of professionalism. The Tin Hat Revue, formed by the Montreal Repertory Theatre, was supported by Imperial Oil. An all-girl group which called itself "The Merry-Go-Round", consisted of twenty-two Toronto debutantes — while another all-girl choir (except for the conductor), was the famous Leslie Bell Singers.

Among the more famous professional artists to perform was Kate Smith, then known as "The Songbird of the South". Older persons will have no difficulty remembering Kate whose vocal rendition of "When The Moon Comes Over The Mountain" and other songs made her name a household word before, during and for years after WWII. Young people will recall that it was the recorded voice of Kate Smith singing "God Bless America" that reputedly inspired the Philadelphia Flyers hockey team to Stanley Cup winning heights a few years ago.

When Kate arrived at Trenton in 1942 she brought with her the popular Columbia Broadcasting System's program of music called "The Spirit of 1942". The show was broadcast from Trenton to a huge North American audience of millions of radio listeners, there being no television then. Before and after the great concert of song and band music, Kate mixed freely among officers and men, increasing her already very high popularity.

Before leaving the base, the star was presented with a gift from the Officers' Mess Committee, the gift being a mysterious looking affair in its wrappings.

"Y'know fellas, there's a story that goes with this gift," Kate explained. "When I was over at the Officers' Mess before the show, I saw a lovely plaque, bearing the inscription — 'Reserved for the Commanding Officer' — and I wanted it badly.

"But your Commanding Officer, Group Captain McGill, explained very diplomatically that I couldn't have it because the plaque has been here ever since the base was established. So I had to settle for this water jug here — and I got it."

Not very long ago, in 1983, Kate Smith, who is now ailing and in a wheelchair, was presented with the Medal of Freedom by President Reagan, the highest civilian honour in the U.S.

When it was announced that Miss Jean Dickenson of Metropolitan Opera and radio fame was to make the first of several visits to Trenton, airmen and airwomen unfamiliar with the appearance of the renowned artist expected to see a prima donna with the traditional battleship build. Instead, they were entertained by a slim, lissome figure — a beauty with a vivid smile, a friendly manner and sparkling personality. The great artist, a lyric soprano, was an immediate hit.

On a visit to the base in 1981, I turned over to the CONTACT editor thousands of photographs taken during the war. One of them was of Carol Bruce who, as explained earlier, was a noted Hollywood actress, a singer and the pinup type of star. She had visited the base and entertained in the fall of 1944. Vivacious and an instant hit, she endeared herself to all and was swamped at the conclusion of her show by the inevitable autograph hunters.

To the editor and others who were looking at the wartime photographs of Carol Bruce, I pointed out that this star is still entertaining us today — as Momma Carlson on the well-known television show, "WKRP in Cincinnati". This bit of news prompted the base, later on, to wonder if I could get in touch with the star and ask for her opinion of her visit. This I was able to do by writing and sending to Miss Bruce in Hollywood some copies of photos and stories of the wartime event.

In a handwritten reply, she wrote that the reminder was like ... "a trip down Memory Lane."

"So many bases," she wrote, "so many people — I only know it was one of the happiest times in my career.

"I have a great affection for Canadians, especially since I started my career at the Mount Royal Hotel as a vocalist.

"I also prize an exquisite crystal and silver powder box, personally engraved, from the Canadian government in recognition of services rendered."

The well-known actor, Hume Cronyn, and actress Ruth Draper were among other popular visitors. Both put on one-person acts. Miss Draper's performance was a particularly memorable one, for she held the stage alone for one-and-a-half hours, presenting entirely new characters in each of her sketches.

Fine recitals were presented now and then by very talented visitors from Toronto's Royal Conservatory of Music, events that were always looked forward to by Trenton's lovers of classical music.

Lovers of classical music also had a great day when the famous Cherniavsky brothers — Jan, pianist, and Mischel, cellist — performed early in 1944. Critics throughout the world had praised the Russian-born brothers to the highest degree, and kings had bestowed honours on them. The skilled duo performed at Trenton only because of a special invitation from the Commanding Officer, G/C A.D. Bell-Irving, an old friend. It was a memorable event.

Quite a number of well-known Canadian professionals entertained at the base — too many to record here. Among some of the more notable, though, were Mart Kenny and his band, and Bert Pearl and Kathleen Stokes of radio's famed "Happy Gang".

Star-studded — that was the entertainment scene at Trenton.

Another niche carved in the annals of Trenton was the opening in 1943 of No. 2 Air Gunners Ground Training School. These trainees are studying component parts of a Browning 303 machine gun.

A third generation of Cairns (Brett) is serving the air force today. Here are the first two: P/O Norman Cairns receives wings at Uplands from his father, W/C D.J.R. Cairns, Trenton's OC of No. 1 K.T.S., in 1943.

Below: Commanding Officer F.S. McGill takes his first salute as an Air Commodore. Acknowledging the salute is W/C J.H. Burden, officer commanding the Composite Training School.

Bottom: The Administration Division of Trenton's Headquarters Staff, December 1942.

Off the Base

If wartime stories of friction between armed forces bases and people in neighbouring towns and villages were true, Trenton had to be an exception. There was a surprisingly good and friendly relationship between the RCAF in the Quinte area and the natives of Trenton, Belleville, Brighton and other nearby towns. It manifested itself in many ways.

Trenton Air Station, with all its sports and social facilities, couldn't begin to meet the demands of so many thousands of airmen and airwomen. It was in this area that neighbouring townspeople came to the rescue. Take dancing, for example. While the base's huge sports hangar could accommodate a large number of dancers, it was never large enough to cope with everybody who wanted to attend. Then, of course, it was only available for dancing now and then — being used on many other nights for other activities such as boxing, badminton, basketball, volleyball and so on.

Belleville was great in helping to solve this problem. The nearest thing to perpetual motion was the town's YMCA Triangle Club. Operating twenty-four hours a day, seven days a week, the club dispensed all the comforts of home and many more. For dancers, there were not only huge Saturday night dances, there was some form of dancing going on almost every night of every week. The Saturday night dances became so popular that the Y's gym could no longer handle the crowds so the events were then moved to the immense floor of the Belleville armouries. Although the sponsors always made sure there were plenty of girls, WDs from the base were welcome. In fact, there was a bit of discrimination in this area. Airmen were charged ten cents admission but girls in uniform were admitted free.

In addition to providing dances, the Y presented picture shows, music appreciation evenings, free bingo, bowling and swimming — even free refreshments.

Those airmen and airwomen whose idea of a pleasant evening consisted of dancing in a different atmosphere would take in one of the Tuesday Night sessions held at the Bay of Quinte Golf and Country Club, overlooking Quinte Bay. The club turned its entire facilities over to air force personnel once every week, a generous move. Couples wishing to sit out the occasional dance were allowed use of a comfortable lounge. All arrangements were directed by various Belleville hospitality clubs and the small admission charge of fifty cents included transportation by chartered bus, refreshments and blanket passes.

The town of Trenton was always ready to match the friendliness and generosity of its larger neighbour. The main organizer of entertainment for the Station's personnel was the Rotary Club which not only held an occasional large bingo on the base, it held regular ones in the town. Considering the sometimes rapid turnover of staff and trainees at the base, the Rotarians must have played host to thousands and thousands of airmen and airwomen during the war — and they must have spent hundreds, perhaps thousands, of dollars on prizes, free cigarettes and refreshments.

I recall that they held a huge Carnival over a three-day holiday period in 1944. Everything was free to armed forces men and women in the vicinity — free bingos, and there were lots of them, free pie feeds and weiner roasts, theatre concerts, draw prizes, etc. — all free.

When on the subject of Trenton's generosity, the Salvation Army deserves a mention. This tiny group would hold bingos in a room over a shop. The prizes were always bright new, shiny fifty-cent pieces. I spent some pleasant evenings with other airmen at these affairs. Like almost every ex-serviceman, I always give to the Sally Ann's annual drive for funds but sometimes feel there is still a lot of ground to make up. I downed great quantities of the Salvation Army's free coffees and doughnuts in Trenton.

At the end of every year, families in the Quinte area would demonstrate their kindness by inviting airmen and airwomen to their homes for Christmas and New Year dinners. In cases where some personnel were not able to get to their own hometowns for either one of the holidays, accommodation in the homes in the Quinte area would sometimes be provided for all five days.

But it wasn't only at Christmas and New Year that citizens welcomed base personnel into their homes. Many a Sunday dinner was shared with men and women from the air station. I was fortunate myself on a number of occasions. CONTACT was printed by the Belleville newspaper — "The Intelligencer" — and the man who set the type and composed the pages for our station paper was Cecil Hardwick. He and his wife invited me to dinner many times and the friendship formed then still exists. On the rare occasions that I'm in the Quinte area these days, I always look up Cec and Babe — and am invariably offered another free meal.

A very nice young lady who worked in The Intelligencer office, Lois Harper, lived in Brighton where her father ran the local hardware store. I can recall at least one invitation to the Harper home for Sunday dinner. Families all over the area would be treating airmen and airwomen to nice homecooked meals.

Getting back to Cecil Hardwick, his generosity was sometimes surprising. On occasion, as I watched him put our paper together, he would look at me and somehow sense correctly that I could do with a beer. This thirst for beer, normally, would not always be easy to quench. Beer was rationed — besides, where might one get a beer anyway in a place like a small printing plant. Also against the possibility was the fact that Cec's boss was a temperance type. Nothing stopped Cec, though. He would go off to a corner of the print shop, drop to his knees as though in prayer, then, from under a type cabinet that reached almost to the floor, would pull out a bottle of beer. He had bottles stashed away in other ingeniously thought-out hiding places. On a particularly hot day, he would cool off his bottles in the Moira River that ran back of the print shop. He should have been running the war.

Earlier mention of Brighton brings to mind an interesting event. The town was holding its annual Fall Fair, which, besides attracting neighbouring townsfolk and farmers, drew a fair number of airmen from the base. One of our NCOs won a live duck in some sort of contest. He brought it back to the base and managed, somehow, to sneak it through the main gate. It appeared next day in the Sergeants' Mess where some characters tried tempting it with dishes of ale — to see what would happen. After a few days the duck mysteriously disappeared and everybody suspected that the cook had something to do with that.

Not all off-base activities involved entertainment and hospitality. Scores of airmen and airwomen left the station several nights a week to attend evening classes at Belleville Collegiate. There, these ambitious types were able to study a wide variety of trades and professions aimed at preparing them to cope with the post-war world. Among the many subjects taught were woodworking, sewing, machine shop work, typing, drafting, motor mechanics and cooking. All the cooking materials were supplied free of charge and the finished cakes, pies, etc. could be eaten on the spot or taken away by those who had made them. Classes in the Collegiate were held four nights a week and the modest three dollar registration fee was refunded at the end of the term if attendance warranted it.

There were other groups of station men and women equally as ambitious but money-mad, as well. A serious shortage of civilian manpower in the area during the war brought requests for help from the base. Many responded. Airmen and airwomen would leave the station after duty hours and work in nearby canneries operated by Crosse and Blackwell, and Stokeley Van Camp. There, our people found the jobs not only profitable but interesting. One night, they might be bottling catsup, husking corn or cleaning tomatoes while on another they would be labeling, packing and shipping. Pay was about fifty cents an hour. The air force people got a certain amount of satisfaction from the work. They thought, rightly, they were doing something worthwhile — for much of what was made was for shipment overseas. Cannery officials claimed they would never have been able to meet their quotas without help from the air force.

Farmers, too, felt the labour shortage. Apple pickers were exceptionally scarce so men and women from Trenton pitched in to help — with a lot of them spending their forty-eight-hour leaves on the job. The pay was usually about fifty cents an hour, although some chaps, full of vigour, made deals that paid them by the barrel.

The best-paying jobs of these service sidelines, though, were at the Belleville docks. Mostly, our men spent weekends there loading and unloading freighters. The work was harder but paid sixty cents or more an hour. To illustrate how hard some of the airmen worked, ten of them once unloaded from a freighter in one evening — 3,200 100-pound bags of sugar and 7,000 cases of beer, a sweet job any way you look at it.

All in all, merchants and farmers in the Quinte area were thankful for the help — and the airmen and airwomen themselves were only too glad to cooperate in what they knew to be necessary work.

I'm not close enough to the base today to judge how its personnel and people in the surrounding areas feel about each other. But copies of the station paper are still sent to me and from them I gather that the friendly cooperative attitude between base and townspeople in the area still exists.

A Potpourri of Memorabilia

Incision Squad

That's right — incision, not precision. This was the name given to a group of aircrew trainees assigned to the station hospital for hernia operations. Many men in the RCAF had been turned down for aircrew because of hernias so the operational plan was beneficial to the air force. While in hospital and convalescing, the men were dressed in what might be termed then as "Zoot-suits of Blue" — light blue, loose-fitting garments. Officially called the "Post-Hermiotomy Convalescent Squad", the men preferred the squad's nickname.

Sports

Sports were always big at Trenton. At one time, a couple of airmen decided to find out how many sports were played on the base and stopped counting after they reached more than twenty. As a result of the tremendous turnover of personnel on the base, a lot of very famous athletes turned up on course and played for station teams. Some hockey names that may be remembered were Roy Conacher, Eddie Wiseman and Tiny Thompson of Boston Bruins, Wally Stanowski and Johnny McCready of the Maple Leafs, Paul Raymond and Johnny Quilty of Montreal Canadiens, and the late Eddie Bush of Detroit Red Wings. Among top baseball players were Art Upper who had played for Toronto's International League Maple Leafs, and Phil Marchildon of Philadelphia "A's", who was later shot down and taken prisoner overseas. Charlie Box, big football and lacrosse star, was on base for quite a while as both staff and trainee. The famous "Torchy" Peden, six-day bicycle racer, was present. There were probably many stars among the RAF chaps. One we recall was Ron Gunner, a professional soccer player with the famous Queen's Park Rangers team.

Blame Trenton

With few exceptions, every station sergeant-major in the RCAF was a product of the "discip school" on the base.

Rationing

Liquor and beer were rationed, as were a number of other commodities almost as important. Soap was in short supply but the base met this shortage with ingenuity. You may not have known it but all that fat and grease left on your plates in various messes was saved. Any of it that could not be sold or made into lard was transformed into soap — a brainwave of the 1942 SAO, W/C C.A. Hoare and Chief Airmen's Mess Cook, F/Sgt Bedard, with an assist from the Flight's grandmother. The Flight remembered a recipe of granny's and, after a little experimenting, he came up with a successful formula that produced 180 pounds of strong, brown floor soap for one dollar. When you realize that the floor of the Airmens' Mess and kitchen were washed every day, often more than once, and there were 8,000 square feet of it, you can imagine the saving made in money. It was figured that cleaning up for several thousands of airmen and airwomen cost two dollars a month. Flight Bedard should have been loaned to Britain. In a letter to the Daily Telegraph, one Briton's answer to the soap shortage was this — "Is it not every true patriot's duty to grow a beard and moustache. He will not only save soap but much valuable time."

Golf

The station now has its own eighteen-hole golf course — but lack of one didn't stop enthusiasts from playing during the war. They teed off at the Trenton and Bay of Quinte courses. Green fees for tournament play were fifty cents — plus a twenty-five-cent fee for prize money. Rubber was in short supply so golfballs were prized. Central Warehouse on the base obtained some reconditioned ones and put them on sale — but buyers had to turn in an old ball to obtain a reconditioned one. Somehow, they coped with the shortage in England but golfers there had other problems. The following new golf rule was introduced: "A ball moved by enemy action may be replaced as near as possible where it lay, or if lost or destroyed, a ball may be dropped not nearer the hole without penalty."

How sweet it was

Base personnel were warned in 1943 that the price for sending a letter within Canada or to the United States was being raised by one cent — to an exhorbitant four cents. Airgraph letters, for posting overseas, were lowered in 1944 to five cents.

Courses

Most airmen and airwomen were familiar with the many courses taught on the base but some courses were little known. One of the most unusual and probably unique in the RCAF was the Court Reporters Course aimed at training a few specially selected airmen to become official stenographers at Courts Martial, a difficult task. The training of firemen was well-

In the 8th Victory Bond Campaign, the unit lowest in sales each day had to care for a family of goats. LAWs Millicent Dudgeon and Joey Grace don't seem to be too unhappy at being losers.

A typical scene on any day. Here S/L L.J. McLeod, examining officer, and S/L J.H. Cooper, chief flying instructor, are shown mapping a flight to be taken on a cross-country hop. Plane in background is a B25 Mitchell Bomber.

Far left: Sgt Peterman, station hospital, shows one of the thousands of turtles that inhabited the base's reedy shore. This one became a WD pet. Left is Nursing Sister F/L Mabell Montgomery, Matron of the Station Hospital. In the King's 1944 New Year's Honours List, she was named an ARRC (Associate of the Royal Red Cross) for her outstanding work.

known but another precedent set on the base was the graduation in 1943 of thirty civilian fire chiefs and deputies from all over Canada. Purpose of the course was to familiarize these men at civilian and service flying schools with the latest methods in firefighting and fire prevention as applicable to the RCAF. Eldest trainee was sixty-four-year-old Thomas Hughes of Calgary.

Digging for Victory

In mid-1944, AFHQ sent out a memorandum asking stations to utilize suitable and available ground to plant "Victory Gardens." This move was aimed at relieving a shortage of fresh vegetables and to ensure that messes had a plentiful supply throughout the season. Trenton went about this job with its usual enthusiasm — on one occasion a bit too enthusiastically. This day, a flight looie, full of patriotism and armed with a hoe, was left by some compatriots to weed the Officers' Mess garden. When they returned, the conscientious gardener proudly displayed what he believed to be the finest crop of weeds ever hoed. You've guessed it. His weeds turned out to be the garden's entire crop of carefully nurtured pumpkins.

Metal shortage

Staff members of the station paper had long become accustomed to receiving material in odd and mysterious ways. The fact that there was a shortage of paperclips was brought home to them when, in 1944, copy for the Women's Division page arrived, neatly clipped together with a bobby pin. Meanwhile, women overseas were having to meet the metal shortage in other ways. Under the heading, "Stretching Things A Bit", we published this little poem...

The ship of state on even keel
Needs tons and tons of corset steel.
The die is set. The law is written.
The ladies now must bulge for Britain.

One-man Shows

We've already described group shows and top professional entertainers who came to Trenton but there were others, individuals mostly, who contributed to the war effort in their own distinctive ways. One such person was Harrison Randle, a self-styled "Cycling Rhythm Maker". Claiming to be able to play 1,800 piano selections from memory, he had already cycled 4,500 miles and covered most bases in eastern Canada when he hit our station in the fall of 1943. Turned down as medically unfit for military service, this chap entertained at all base messes, canteens and lounges before moving on his lonely way to other bases. Another one-man act was Pat Gibson, brother of "Hoot", the famous filmstar, who put on a sort of western show. He was supported by his dog "Chum", who also happened to be a half-brother to the first of the famous "Lassies".

The rout completed

All the old sweats who resented the enlistment of women into the armed forces choked on their beer when it was announced, in early 1944, that a "Beauty Salon" was being built for the Trenton WDs. It featured — mygawd! — shampooing, finger waving and haircutting, and specialized in "styles suited to the wearing of uniforms without losing the feminine touch."

A gabby lot

In early 1944, a "Forum Amicorum" was organized on the base, its aim being "the maintenance of general interest in current events and the study and discussion of postwar plans, social reforms, etc." In spite of its highfaluting name, it was not the first such group at Trenton. AFHQ encouraged discussion groups but we wonder if it took into consideration the always abundant enthusiasm which Trentonians put into everything. By mid-1944, there were seventeen discussion groups operating from Headquarters, Maintenance Wing, KTS and FIS staffs.

Ladybirds

Women were not enlisted to fly in the RCAF during WWII but a very few who taught at civilian-operated Elementary Flying Training Schools had to first pass a flying instructors' test at Trenton. Three of these were a Miss Gillies, Marion Orr and Violet Millstead. Marion Orr, who was tested at the base in mid-1942, went on to teach, then joined the Air Transport Auxiliary overseas. There, she flew Spitfires, Hurricanes, Hudsons, Mosquitoes, Ansons, Lysanders and many lesser-known types. In 1982, she was made a member of Canada's prestigious Aviation Hall of Fame. When in touch with her not long ago, she was still flying and teaching at sixty-five years of age. Her flying hours total a staggering 22,000. She instructs with the Trenton civilian flying club today.

Trenton's Flying Cairns

In the 1914-18 war, young Jimmy Cairns joined the Royal Flying Corps and later became an expert and instructor in aerial photography. In the early part of WWII he was a Wing Commander at Trenton in command of the KTS School of Administration. In 1943 he traveled to RCAF Station, Uplands to pin wings on his son, Norman, who had graduated from the SFTS with distinction. In 1981, I saw Norm at Trenton's giant 50th Anniversary Air Show — looking up at a modern jet being put through its paces for the benefit of 100,000 spectators. The pilot? Norm's son — and Jimmie's grandson — Brett, continuing a family service in Canada's Air Forces of more than sixty years.

A Potpourri of Memorabilia / 137

This amphibian used to turn up at Trenton for repairs. Known officially as a WALRUS, the Navy had other names for its ugly, useful ship — some semi-derogatory, others semi-affectionate.

A constant source of amazement to most airmen was the enormous number of books and precis that School of Administration trainees were required to tote around. This group of officers are marching into a classroom for a session of study.

Airwomen surrendering? Unfortunately, no. These were WD P.T.I. trainees doing some outdoor exercising. In outfits like these, they formed another in a long list of unofficial attractions.

Billy Bates, one of 60 chefs, tells a tall story to some of the messmen-and-women (there were 120) as they took a well-deserved rest on the Mess Hall lawn.

Nothing too good for the air force

In 1943, as a result of much evidence of foot trouble on sick parades, the station hospital sent Cpl Woods to St. Thomas to study about the care of feet and the proper fitting of boots and shoes. In 1944, the base had a fully-trained orthopedist on staff. We wonder if the infantry received such care.

Thumbs up!

The problem of using the railway as a means of transportation loomed large in the eyes of an AC2 Standard Group, at $1.30 per day, of which sixty cents was deducted for dependants. With a bi-monthly pay amounting to $9.50 from which one had to deduct money for cleaning, laundry, smokes, shoe polish, etc., a trip even to Toronto at $3.05 was just about out of the question. So it was thumbs up on the King's Highway. However, an AFHQ ruling forbidding the practice of hitchhiking came into effect. But as long as there were lamps in windows, sons and daughters will find a way home — in spite of snow, rain, sleet, hail or Air Force Routine Orders. It remained for the tiny village of Aurora to do something about the problem. It erected a cozy little building at each highway entrance where homesick airmen and airwomen could wait for kindly motorists. Not to be outdone, Trenton's Rotary Club presented, on behalf of the Cross & Blackwell Co., two similar huts, each with a sign attracting the attention of motorists. One hut was placed at each end of the town. The huts were officially received on behalf of airmen and airwomen by the CO at a ceremony in the Sports Hangar — an indication of what was thought, from the top to the bottom, of the AFHQ regulation against holding up the old thumb.

E for Effort

Some of the trainees at Trenton's Motor Transport School were so anxious to make the grade they sometimes embellished their stories of previous civilian experience with more than little white lies. One student informed his instructor that he had been with Greyhound Lines for four years, with Smith Transport for five years, with Imperial Oil for four years and spent two years as a private chauffeur. When asked by the instructor how old he was, the student replied, "Eighteen!"

Food, Glorious Food!

In early 1944, Trenton's mess halls were preparing food, daily, for between 7,000 and 8,000 meals. Personnel were eating a ton of potatoes every day and 2,400 eggs, while making milk disappear at the rate of 180 gallons daily. Meals were planned a week in advance and sixty chefs and 120 messmen and women were necessary to cook and serve them.

A hospital happening

On September 1, 1940, the first operation at the station hospital, and the first ever at any RCAF hospital, was performed. A patient suffering from acute appendicitis was on hand. After consultation among doctors it was decided to operate on him, even though there were few instruments for the job. A writer for CONTACT reported that the patient had a look of complacency as a mask was put over his face and the anaesthetic administered. New to the station, he thought surgery at Trenton was a regular occurrence. He may have worn a different look had he realized he was helping to make history at the base.

Khaki at Trenton

The hospital item is a reminder that all was not air force blue on the base. Summer drill uniforms were khaki, of course, but there were army khaki uniforms to be seen all year around and throughout the war. The hospital, for example, was administered by the Royal Canadian Army Medical Corps until the fall of 1940 when all members of the RCAMC attached to the air force became members of the RCAF. The Royal Canadian Army Service Corps looked after the station's food requirements — and the Royal Canadian Army Dental Corps the care of teeth — right up until after the war. Another group in khaki were men of the Canadian Postal Corps who served until just after mid-1943 when they were posted (if you'll excuse the pun) off the base and replaced by airwomen.

Another first

The first baptismal service was held during a church parade on June 11, 1944 when the son and daughter of F/Sgt Herb Wilkinson and Mrs. Wilkinson were baptized, with F/L Padre Ross Cameron officiating.

Trenton - Hollywood of the North

In an earlier chapter I made brief reference to "the little-known-about motion picture industry in the town during the early 1900s." Not many persons in the town, nor who went throught the base, may be aware that it was the Ontario Government which chose Trenton for the location of its motion picture studio. Many "shorts" were made there — with more elaborate productions following. Tyrone Power, father of the famous Hollywood movie star, made "The Great Shadow" at the Trenton studio. Some time later, the no-less-famous Bruce Bairnsfather, mentioned in my cartoon story, spent half-a-million dollars to produce his "Carry On Sergeant" feature film at Trenton.

Epilogue

My stay at Trenton was longer than most — four years. During that time, the base became, for me, more than a place to work. With no family in civilian life, it seemed more like a home. Yet after the war, caught up in the competitive business world, I visited Trenton only once during the next thirty-six years.

This was as a member of a press party, flown to the station in September 1949 to report on presentation of the Memorial Gates, a gift to Canada from the governments of the United Kingdom, Australia and New Zealand.

In 1981, the base celebrated its 50th Anniversary. Word went out that its information officer and others were interested in contacting anybody who could contribute material, anecdotes or photographs of help in compiling a history of the station. As owner of every wartime copy of CONTACT and WINGS bound into hardcover volumes and with thousands of wartime photographs and other Trenton memorabilia, I responded — and so began a new association with the base.

Invited to Trenton prior to its great 1981 Homecoming Celebrations, I was surprised to find that CONTACT, which had ceased publication in late 1945, had been revived in the late sixties and was still going strong. Not only that, it was using some of my old wartime articles. I was asked to return to the base for the Homecoming and set up a display of my books and photographs for the interest of visitors.

This I did. Many persons who knew me and of my work during the war years were at the Homecoming. There were renewed friendships and new friendships made. Apart from this and the many planned activities, being back at the old station was for many of us a source of happiness. To see the hangars, hear the planes, to walk around the barrack blocks and to see the fine old Administration Building being spruced up — all of this made nostalgia a common emotion on Homecoming weekend.

At the conclusion of activities, I was invited to contribute again to the station paper. Reluctant at first, because of my long absence from air force affairs, I eventually sent some articles in which I tied in present-day events with things that happened on the base about forty years before. Would today's young Trenton people be interested, I wondered?

Assured that they are, the idea for this book took shape. Many of you who served in Canada or overseas must have gone through Trenton, for no other base trained so many persons in such a variety of trades. It is my hope, then, that this attempt to describe some of the on-duty and off-duty activities at the great wartime base will help fill a void in the publishing of books about the RCAF. In writing the stories, there was always the feeling that so many events and tales of so many people were being left out. Many of you must have memories which you feel are worthy of publication. Yet a book of encyclopedic-size would not be big enough to report on all wartime off-duty activities that took place at Trenton, let alone include a full story of the important training that went on there.

In his trans-Canada telephone interview during the base's Fiftieth Anniversary celebrations, Eric Nicol described Trenton as "a handsome station" — and it was that. Persons who were at the base before, during and after the war would, today, find many things the same — for the permanent tall barrack blocks, Mess hall buildings and others are still there. But, unfortunately, automobiles, which seem to be everywhere, have brought about some regrettable changes.

Gone are the beautiful flower beds cared for so lovingly by F/Sgt White, in his spare time. And the main parade square that fronts the impressive old Administration Building (a sacred area, in some ways), is now often used as just another car parking lot. One wonders what poor old SWO John Silver would think, were he alive today.

Regardless of the omissions, it is my hope the book has revived some pleasant memories. Trenton was a fine station — and still is. It is easy to remember it and the friends made there, with affection. Even during the war, many men and women who had left Trenton for other bases in Canada or overseas used to write letters to CONTACT expressing their admiration for the base. Absence made their hearts grow fonder then — and probably still does, today.

Treat yourself, sometime, to a visit to the base on one of its great annual Air Force Days which are open to the public and which regularly draw crowds from 70,000 to 100,000. No other Canadian air show, in the air or on the ground, matches the one at Trenton.

Author's Note:
In the chapter headed, "Musing About The Muse", reference is made to the epic poem "High Flight". For the benefit of those who loved that poem but whose memory of it has become dimmed by time, here it is in its entirety and as it was used on a beautiful poster advertising Trenton's 1984 Air Show.

High Flight

Oh, I have slipped the surly bonds of earth
 And danced the skies on laughter-silver wing;
Sunward I've climbed, and joined the tumbling mirth
Of sun-split clouds - and done a hundred things
You have not dreamed of - wheeled and soared and swung
High in the sunlit silence. Hov'ring there
I've chased the shouting wind along, and flung
My eager craft through footless halls of air.
Up, up the long delirious, burning blue
I've topped the windswept heights with easy grace
Where never lark or even eagle flew.
And, while with silent, lifting mind I've trod
The high untrespassed sanctity of space,
Put out my hand, and touched the face of God.

P/O J.G. Magee, Jr. RCAF

Acknowledgements:

The author is grateful to the following...
Captain Earl Hewison and other officers of Canadian Forces Base, Trenton for their interest and encouragement ... the Base for permission to reproduce information and illustrations from World War II issues of the RCAF, Trenton station magazine, CONTACT ... Joan Wright, a recent CONTACT editor, whose publishing of some of my recent stories led to the writing of this collection.

John Bellinger and Dennis (Bud) Nock, former associates of mine at Maclean Hunter Limited, for helpful advice regarding graphic presentation and photo reproduction.

The many ex-RCAF friends — and others — who thought this book should be written and whose persistent needling helped bring it to completion.

J.W. (Bill) Sargent